Dedication

I would like to dedicate this book to the memory and honour of Sister Gwen Shaw, my mother in the spirit, my mentor, my friend. I never could get enough of her.

I would also like to dedicate it to all of the End-Time Handmaidens and Servants on the planet, those who have already gone on to their reward, and those who are just awakening to the call. I am here for you. I am your handmaiden. The Lord put me here to serve you, and by His grace I trust that I will be a blessing to you. I pray that the Lord will inspire you to serve Him diligently by means of this book.

Table of Contents

TABLE OF CONTENTS (CONTINUED)

TABLE OF CONTENTS (CONTINUED)

FOREWORD

These Last Days continue to spawn a multitude of new "Christian" ministries. Understandably, inquiring minds are not content to "read just the book cover." They want to probe their credibility. Gazing admiringly at a magnificent high rise tower, few people turn their thoughts to the foundation lying buried under that superstructure. Yet for a prospective property buyer, it is the unseen part that should decide his offer price for the visible part.

The world-wide ministry of the End-Time Handmaidens And Servants International has been impacting human lives and nations over some four decades now. Its roots, its credibility, lie in the Spirit of the phenomenal woman God directed to establish and build it — Dr. Gwen Shaw. When it was time for her to pass the torch to a successor, it is little wonder that God would direct her to appoint someone whom she had watched over as God, under her very eyes (and hands), shaped, sharpened and passed though His tempering furnace.

Kind produces after its kind. Would it be an accident to find that the new President and Vice-President share Sister Gwen's passion and vision for missionary evangelism, for simplicity, for empathy with suffering peoples of the earth, for God's Covenant People Israel, for composing, playing and singing inspiring music? Would it be strange to see in them the same solidity of faith in God, depth of knowledge of His word and a never-satisfied love for the Lord?

This book will give the reader "a peek behind the End-Time Handmaidens and Servants curtains." It will challenge you not only to stand with End-Time Handmaidens and Servants but also to meaningfully pray with love for the new leadership stepping into the enormous shoes of Sister Gwen.

I personally count it a great honor from God to write this foreword. Having met Sister Gwen Shaw in 1968 and working with her over the years, I marvel at the Divine Wisdom that has directed this ministry transition, and you will too!

— Apostle Emmanuel Jibuike

Sharon Buss
President

Philip Buss
Vice President

Introduction

On January 13, 2013 at 1:30 p.m., our dearly beloved leader, mother, sister and cherished friend, Sister Gwen Shaw, passed into Glory from her home. The peace of the Lord was present in her room for days, and we felt the saints and angels present to usher her across to her heavenly home. The funeral took place on January 22 and with it we began counting thirty days of Holy Convocation to celebrate how the Lord Jesus Christ used Sister Gwen throughout her 88 years of life.

We had spent thirty days celebrating Papa Jim's life when he passed away March 5, 2007. When I saw in the scriptures that the Children of Israel spent a thirty-day period of mourning in the wilderness for Aaron and they repeated it again when Moses passed into the Presence of the Lord, I purposed in my heart that we must do this for Sister Gwen.

We had some wonderful ministers stand in our pulpit who helped to carry us in the spirit and comforted us as we mourned together our loss of a great general in the army of God. Sister Gwen's life was an inspiration to thousands upon thousands. Only Heaven knows the number.

It was a glorious time and much needed. Nothing could have been more important in those first days of transition than to simply stop and wait on the Lord. His Presence in the meetings was so awesome that some started talking about the possibility of continuing after the thirty days were finished. I took a deep breath and said, "If the Glory Cloud becomes visible (as it was in the Azusa Street Revival in the early 1900's), then we'll know that's the sign that we are to continue." Although we sensed the Glory of the Presence of

1

the Lord, it didn't become visible to us at that time. We are still expecting it to happen though, and when it does, we will stop again and simply wait on God, ready to do any command He gives us.

One week after the funeral, I received an email from Harold McDougal, publisher for Ruth Heflin's books and many others. He had attended the funeral and brought a beautiful tribute to Sister Gwen at the convocation. In part, he wrote:

"On amazon.com, I see many pages of Gwen's books but none of yours. On the ETH site, I see only one small item. Now that you have taken the torch, you need at least one solid book of your own. Many have told me that the best thing I could have done for Jane Lowder [Ruth Heflin's successor] was to publish her story, *High and Lifted Up*, and now we're working on another title for her. What I visualize is something like your life story, climaxing with Sister Gwen's passing and burial and you taking the reins of the ministry. Such a book could go a long way to assure everyone who loved her that the vision will not die."

I had never dreamed of writing my story. I'm only 55—I thought that people only wrote their memoirs when they retired and had the time to do so, or if they were running for a major political office. But Brother McDougal's words kept ringing in my spirit. And although time was getting away from me with all the activities of keeping the ministry going, I felt I must attempt this feat.

So if I'm 55, then I am halfway to the age of 110, and I have lived long enough to have seen God's hand lovingly, faithfully, and mercifully orchestrating the minutest details of life all around me to bring me to this day. Sister Gwen Shaw has graduated to her Heavenly Home and left me in charge of the End-Time Handmaidens and Servants International. I have served the Lord with her for nearly 36 years. Only Heaven will reveal all the details preparing me for this moment, but I know that I was born for this. The circumstances of my life were orchestrated by God to prepare me. I am amazed at the wonderful hand of God preparing Sister Gwen's successor before she even founded the ministry. How great is our God! How marvelously He works! I trust that you will agree as you read the story of my life thus far.

Acknowledgements

The biggest thank you goes to my dear, sweet husband, Philip Buss, who has lived the last 32 years of this story with me. Thank you for your patience with me, for proofreading, and for helping me find photos to insert. I wish I would have had time and room to use them all!

Thank you to the rest of the proofreaders: Rona Spiropoulos, Marilyn Hargis, Judith Moore, Carol Cotner, Geri Trees, Cheryl Courreges, and Doreen Shurley.

A special thank you to Joy Kusek for the beautiful cover design and final proofreading.

Thank you to my dad, Rev. Edwin Cooper, who helped me get the details right for the account of my roots and early stages. I love you, Dad!

Thank you to my dear elder sister, Carole, who sent me the right direction to find Jesus as my Saviour, and who first invited me to come and hear the "Bible smugglers." Without your obedience to God and prayers on my behalf, I would not be where I am today.

"You Will Take Her Place
When She's Gone"

"You will take her place when she's gone," said the Voice I heard inside me. I fell to my knees, weeping. Sister Gwen Shaw, the Founder and President of the End-Time Handmaidens, Inc., was preaching under a mighty anointing at the ministry's First World Convention in Dogpatch, Arkansas. I was sitting in the front row, directly in front of the pulpit in the Marble Falls Convention Center, taking it all in like a hungry baby bird in the nest, just waiting for its mommy to feed it.

I hung on to every word that was preached throughout those meetings held during the Memorial Day weekend in 1976. I was eighteen years old and just two weeks from graduating from high school. My whole life was ahead of me. I was planning to go to the music school at Western Michigan University; I even had some scholarships to help me. What was God saying? What was I to do?

God has a plan for the life of every person on the planet. Sadly, the vast majority seldom wake up to their place in God's plan, although, when we look back over our shoulder from Heaven's point of view, we can see how many times He has used us without our even knowing it. Had we known it, we might have become proud, so He wisely hides our accomplishments from ourselves. Heaven will reveal so much that is unseen here. I plan to spend a lot of time in the "video replay" department when I get there so I can see what was unseen to our natural eyes! And how much of what was going on around us in the unseen was orchestrated by God to prepare us for events yet to come?

Romans 8:28 is so powerful! "And we know that all things work together for good to them that love God, to them who are the called according to his purpose." I believe that our Heavenly Father planned everything out before He even said, "Let there be light," knowing all of the good choices, bad choices, and stupid choices that every person who would ever live would make. He arranged that out there ahead of us, something or someone would be in exactly the right place at exactly the right time so that each circumstance would all work together for the good of those who love Him and are the called according to His purpose. My story is filled with Romans 8:28 moments, as I'm sure yours is as well. But it really begins before my birth.

Generational Calling: Dad

My father, Edwin Raymond Cooper was born and raised with his two brothers on a dairy farm in McBain, Michigan. His father, John Ira Cooper, was a progressive farmer, always anxious to learn new techniques. He was the first in the area to use a tractor. Dad's mother, Betsey VanderVeen Cooper, was a second generation Dutch girl that was born in Michigan. Her grandparents came over from the Netherlands. Her grandfather was a very godly man. He knew his Bible and taught Bible verses to his grandchildren in the Dutch language. He had a vision of Heaven on the day he died.

Dad grew up in a Christian home, and they were church-goers. When he was high school age, while working on the farm during thrashing time, he was heading for the thrashing machine with a load of grain. A storm came up and lightning struck the ground not very far from where he was. Dirt flew up in the air from the impact. He knew that according to the laws of electricity the lightning should have hit him or the horses instead of the ground. After unloading the grain, he put the horses in the barn and prayed his first earnest prayer of thanks that he wasn't hit, and that the Lord spared his life. From that time on he took his relationship with the Lord seriously.

His church, Rehoboth Reformed Church in Lucas, Michigan, had a pastor that was very strong for missions, and was earnestly praying that his church would raise up a missionary.

In answer to that pastor's prayers, Dad heard the call of the Lord early in his college career while he was going to Michigan State College, in East Lansing. Some of the young men in his co-op house had regular Bible studies that he enjoyed. They went to Intervarsity Christian Fellowship, so he went too. Intervarsity had a strong emphasis on missions. He attended classes with other young men who were studying to be agricultural missionaries. It was in this environment the call began to incubate in his spirit. When a paper was sent around in his college class that asked if there was anyone interested in agricultural missions, he signed that he was. He was then asked, "What denomination are you from?" When he replied the Reformed Church in America, he soon received a letter from the mission board asking him to contact them for further information.

He learned that there were good opportunities for agricultural missionaries in lands that were not open to the Gospel—the good news that Jesus, God's Son, sacrificed Himself to pay the penalty of eternal suffering for our wrongdoings.

Mom's Calling

My mother, Elaine Marie Parks Cooper, was born and raised in Detroit, Michigan. Her father, Walter J. Parks, was also a Detroiter. He graduated from eighth grade and became an electrician's apprentice. He learned the trade and beyond. The only time he ever went to college was to teach. I understand that he designed the lighting for Cobo Hall in Detroit, the Ambassador Bridge to Canada, and Crisler Arena at the University of Michigan in Ann Arbor. Mom's mother, Dorothy

Marie Covert Parks was raised in Clio, Michigan. Her father was a teacher and took advanced training in various places, so they travelled some. Some of her ancestors were among the first to settle Gennesse County, Michigan.

Mom attended Bob Jones University for two years, spanning the time the campus moved from Cleveland, Tennessee to Greenville, South Carolina. While studying there, she learned to eat Southern food and added that to our Northern table as I was growing up. Eating grits and other Southern delicacies as a child helped prepare me to live most of my adult life in Arkansas.

Apparently the accommodations in the new dormitories weren't as good as they had been in the previous location and Mom commented on that fact. Grandma Covert, her mother's mother, was living with the family at the time, and she took it upon herself to write a letter to the school to complain about it. As I understand the story, someone from the school wrote back a message something like: "If your granddaughter doesn't like it here, she doesn't have to come back!"

I'm sure that there were tears and words of consternation in the household, but I understand that Grandpa took the situation in hand and made arrangements for Mom to attend Michigan State College in East Lansing, Michigan. There she joined the Intervarsity Christian Fellowship and played the pump organ for their services.

Their Love Story

Intervarsity held a banquet each year, and the students were encouraged to come as couples. Mom didn't have a date. Someone thought of Dad and gave him Mom's phone number. Dad knew who she was, since she was the organist, but she didn't know him. He called her and invited her out for coffee. He told her that he was asked to accompany her to the banquet, and she agreed.

8

After the banquet, they began to go to church together quite often. After some time, Mom called home and told Grandma that she was going to break up with him after church that Sunday evening. She really liked him, but knew she had a call of God on her life and couldn't let him come between her and God's Plan.

On Sunday evening, she and Dad were having coffee and he said to her, "I'm called to be a missionary. I wonder if you would be my wife and we'd be a missionary couple. The field will probably be Africa."

She told him through her tears, "I didn't think you were called to be a missionary, but now that I know you are, the answer is yes!" Then she began to tell him about her calling.

When she called home and told Grandma the news, "You're going to get married?!" was all that Grandpa could hear of the conversation.

"Wait until I see that young man! I'll tell him a thing or two." Grandpa began to fuss, thinking the worst. Of course he simmered down when he heard the rest of the story. He didn't know about her plan to break up with him, so he jumped to the wrong conclusion.

Grandpa and Grandma Parks, Mom and Dad, Grandma and Grandpa Cooper

They were married June 30, 1950, just two weeks after they graduated from Michigan State and five days after Mom's twenty-second birthday. They moved to Peck, Michigan (in the "thumb" of the state) where Dad taught agriculture to WWII veterans. My brother, Paul was born the following May.

They wrote to the mission boards of both their denominations and only the Reformed Church in America had positions for agricultural missionaries. Another couple had applied at the same time as Mom and Dad, and the other couple was sent to Africa. Mom and Dad were selected to go to India.

Agricultural Missionaries in India

They moved to New Brunswick, New Jersey, where Dad attended Biblical Seminary in New York. At the seminary he was instructed in linguistics to learn pronunciation by a missionary who had retired from India. My brother, John was born there a year and a week after Paul. In 1952, they sailed for India.

Mom and Dad with John and Paul before sailing to India

After a year of language school in Kodaikanal, the "hill station" where the American boarding school and hospital were, they were posted on the plains in a place called "The Farm," in Katpadi, in what was then called Madras State, now called Tamil Nadu, in Southern India. It was a place where agriculture was taught to the local farmers. He continued language study there.

Dad at the pulpit in the mission chapel

A farmer in the United States had a huge egg incubator that was powered by electricity, and he decided that he wanted a bigger one, so he donated this one to Dad's mission. Dad was involved with getting it running and productive. He had had a course in electrical wiring in college, and it came in handy then.

One of Dad's poultry projects involved trading their chickens that had been inoculated against the local diseases to help the villagers to have healthier stock.

Mom dressed in a sari

They would then slaughter the uninoculated local chickens they received in trade and sold them in the market, thus removing the chickens that were susceptible to disease.

When the weather became too unbearably hot on the plains, the missionaries came to cool off in Kodaikanal because of its higher elevation. On May 30, 1955, my sister Carole was born in that town. Paul and John stayed with Mom in our Kodai home when they started their schooling, while Dad continued working on the plains about 300 miles away. They were still too young for boarding school.

John, Carole, and Paul — I'm the bundle

As they were nearing the end of their first five-year term, they had to delay their plans for going home to America because they discovered that I was on the way. The doctor projected that I would be born on April Fool's Day, but I fooled them and came two weeks later on April 14, 1958. Dad told me that Mom laughed when the doctor told her, "It's a girl!" I was born in the same room as Carole.

Nine weeks later, we sailed for the States. They brought me home in a

The Coopers sail home from India

12

market basket. We were coming home for their year of furlough, itinerating and all of the things you do when you come home from the mission field, intending to go back.

Back in Michigan

When we got settled in Holland, Michigan, we all had to have physicals which included TB (tuberculosis) tests. Mine was positive, although no one else's in the family was. When they did a chest x-ray, they found scar tissue, evidence that I had already been healed. I guess the devil was trying to take me out and God would not let him, Glory to God.

My folks intended to go back to India but the mission board decided to deny their return due

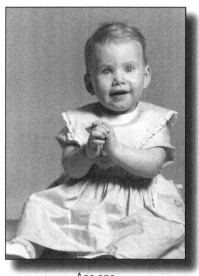

Age one

to my mother's weight. She had been heavy from the time that she had surgery as a child to remove her tonsils and adenoids.

My Dad was particularly devastated by this setback. My grandmother once described him to me as "a ship without a sail" during that time. He went to work for Grandpa Parks, my mother's father, and we grew up as a semi-ordinary Christian family but my parents burned in their hearts to serve God on the mission field.

It is interesting to me that my father felt the call to Africa and my mother felt called to Eastern Europe, and they went to India. God is good. Perhaps that is part of what set me up for a vision for all nations.

Daddy's Girl

I think that my sisters and I were all "Daddy's girls." But Mom made an agreement with Dad that it was his turn to be the one to get up in the night with this one. After three babies ahead of me, she was ready for a break! Consequently, one of my earliest recollections (and one that Dad continually reminds me of), is that if I woke up in the night, I would come in and tap him on the arm saying, "Daddy, I had a dweam. Would you wock-a-bye me?" To which request, my dear, kind, patient

Age four

Daddy would get out of bed, grab his magnetic flashlight that he kept attached to the metal bedframe, and take me to the rocking chair in the living room. I don't really know how often it happened, but I know it must have been fairly frequently, as I remember it happening in the cottage on Lake Chemung where we lived until I was five and then in the Byron Road house. I remember at times I had to wake him up to take me back to bed!

Sometimes at bedtime he hummed Brahms' lullaby, ending with his own words for the last line, "and my little girl's going to sleep." Sometimes he sang, "When He Cometh."

When He cometh, when He cometh
To make up His jewels,
All His jewels, precious jewels,
His loved and His own.

Like the stars of the morning,
His bright crown adorning,
They shall shine in their beauty,
Bright gems for His crown.

14

Little children, little children,
Who love their Redeemer,
Are the jewels, precious jewels,
His loved and His own.
—William O. Cushing/George F. Root

A few years ago, when chatting with him, I mentioned a recollection of mine that when he was rocking me to try and get me to take a nap while visiting at Grandma and Grandpa Parks' house, he stopped in the middle of the song. I said to him, "Daddy, you forgot to say, 'deemer!" When I told him my recollection, he began to laugh and said that he used to do that deliberately because he thought my reaction was so cute! Apparently it must have happened often enough that I remembered it.

Evidently I wasn't always completely awake in those night visits and began a habit of walking in my sleep. I actually remember a conversation that I had in the night that was enough to wake me up when my dreaming made me want to go down to the basement—this wasn't a good thing from my parents' point of view since the entrance to the basement was outside the back door! One more move across town cured me of sleep walking, though, as the room I shared with my sister was at the top of the second-storey stairs. One good tumble down to the landing (which I don't remember because I was asleep) put an end to my sleep walking!

Another memorable activity was Dad reading to Carole and me (we shared a room) at bedtime from a Bible Story book that was illustrated like a comic book. He would then work with us on memorizing things like the Lord's Prayer, the books of the Bible, or portions of scripture like the Beatitudes, the Ten Commandments and the 23rd Psalm. I'm very grateful to the Lord for all the good foundation in the Word that my Dad built in me.

School Days

A US Supreme Court ruling banned organized prayer and Bible reading from the public school in 1962, and I started school in 1963. Mine was one of the first classes that was affected by the ruling from the start. In spite of it, though, Mrs. Withey, my kindergarten teacher, had us recite the Lord's Prayer each day along with the Pledge of Allegiance.

I also had the "privilege" of being among the first unsuspecting "Guinea pigs" to experience the "New Math," that mysterious method of teaching math principles instead of math facts, hoping that kids could figure it out for themselves. The theory was that students would retain the resulting facts better because they had come up with the answers on their own. It was an experiment in US public schools that lasted about ten years until it was morphed into something a bit more understandable. Parents complained that they couldn't help their children do their homework because they couldn't understand it.

During first grade, I was absent due to sickness and one of my siblings brought my school work home to me. Apparently some new algebraic concept was taught while I was sick, and I didn't understand how to do the worksheet that I received. The problem on the page was $7 - \Delta = 4$. We had only been working on addition problems up to that point, and I didn't understand subtraction yet. I kept trying different numbers in the triangle, and ended up erasing a hole in the paper. I must have made an inner vow at that point to not like math. I managed to get A's in it most of the time all through school, but I never liked it. I enjoyed all my other classes.

Becoming a Believer

When I was in first grade, age six, both of my maternal great-grandmothers passed away within a few months of each other. Some months after Grandma Covert died, I was looking

16

at the little folder in her memory that the funeral home provides. I asked my sister, Carole, "Do you think Grandma Covert is an angel yet?"

"That's not how it works. You'd better go talk to Mom" she replied, in her older sisterly way.

So I went to Mom and she explained to me that we all have sinned and done things that we shouldn't, and that those sins would keep us away from God. Jesus came to be the sacrifice to pay the penalty for our sins, so that we could be able to go to Heaven if we would accept His gift of salvation. She helped me pray and ask God to forgive me of my sins and to ask Jesus to come and live in my heart. When I prayed that prayer, I felt wonderful! I couldn't wait to tell others about Him! I wanted to "go forward" in church and tell the pastor about it. The next Sunday when we were in church, I begged to be allowed to tell about my experience in the opening part of the primary Sunday School classes. Only one other child had ever heard about asking Jesus to come into her heart. I encouraged my classmates to pray.

Shortly after this I received a postcard from the pastor, inviting me to join his class for baptism and membership. So I took the card to my Dad and he told me that I had already been baptized when I was a baby. He patiently explained to me that in Acts 16:25-34, when the Philippian jailer was saved and his whole house, it is assumed that there were babies in his house, so the whole household got baptized at one time. This is where the doctrine of infant baptism started. I was very disappointed at the time, but this delay was of the Lord.

Family Devotions

I am so grateful that our parents provided a solid foundation of faith for us in our home. Every evening we sat down after dinner to have devotions. We began with a song; each one of us in turn getting to choose what to sing. It would always be the first verse of a hymn and we had a pretty good repertoire. My favorite was, "Throw Out the Lifeline." Children seem to love doing motions when singing, so when we sang that one, I pretended to be fishing, reeling in the lifeline. (I think I drove my brothers crazy with that one—but then I think I annoyed them a lot, being the "punk-kid" little sister.)

Following the song, Dad would always read to us. On alternating nights he would read a passage of scripture or from a missionary story. I remember sitting on his lap many a night, being absorbed in stories from the mission field. He read from Paul White's *Jungle Doctor* series—probably all of them, I think, about the adventures of a missionary doctor in what was then called Tanganyika. *An Angel at Her Shoulder*, by Lillian Dickson, about her experiences as a missionary in Taiwan, then called Formosa. *The Dayuma Story*, Rachel Saint's story of how she continued to reach out to bring the Gospel to the Auca/Waodani people that had killed her brother Nate and the other four missionaries in Ecuador in 1955. (Dad calls them the "heroes of his generation.").

Called by God

So you can see how the ground of my heart was plowed and fertile to receive the seed of the calling of God. When I was in the third grade, I was in the Junior Choir at the First Baptist Church in Howell. Mrs. Joanne Clark was the director. One of the songs that we learned from the Singspiration hymnal was, "So Send I You."

So send I you to labor unrewarded,
To serve unpaid, unloved, unsought, unknown,
To bear rebuke, to suffer scorn and scoffing-
So send I you to toil for Me alone.

18

TAKE THE LID OFF

So send I you to bind the bruised and broken,
O'er wand'ring souls to work, to weep, to wake,
To bear the burdens of a world aweary-
So send I you to suffer for My sake.

So send I you to loneliness and longing,
With heart ahung'ring for the loved and known,
Forsaking home and kindred, friend and dear one-
So send I you to know My love alone.

So send I you to leave your life's ambition,
To die to dear desire, self-will resign,
To labor long, and love where men revile you-
So send I you to lose your life in Mine.

So send I you to hearts made hard by hatred,
To eyes made blind because they will not see,
To spend, tho' it be blood, to spend and spare not-
So send I you to taste of Calvary.
—Margaret Clarkson

My heart was captivated! I knew that God was calling me to be a missionary. For some time I was determined to become a missionary doctor like Jungle Doctor—he was my hero! Dad told me about how Dr. Ida Scudder had taken me in her arms and blessed me when I was a baby. I wouldn't be surprised if she had said something like, "Lord, let this child grow up to serve You as a missionary!" "Dr. Ida" was a third generation missionary to India through the Reformed Church in America, the same mission board that sent my parents. She had received the call of God on her life as a young woman when visiting India when her mother was ill (Ida didn't want to live in India). In one evening, three men individually came to their door, each saying that his wife was dying in childbirth and asked if she could come to help. She replied that she wasn't qualified, but her father was a doctor and he could help. They each in turn sadly said, "No man can see my wife. She will have to die." Ida

Scudder didn't sleep that night. She returned to America and became a doctor, then went back to India and built a hospital and medical school for women. With her blessing I had good reason to think I might become a missionary doctor.

As a senior in High school I was at the top of my class in Anatomy and Physiology, even beating out the next highest in a "bone bee," although he really was better equipped to become a doctor (and did), because he could do the Chemistry, Physics, and Calculus classes that I opted out of for lack of interest! I preferred music at that point. The closest I got to a medical career was becoming an Emergency Medical Technician in 1978, and working on the Newton County Volunteer Ambulance Service for about two and a half years. I was too young to drive the Ambulance, so I had to be the one on the team to administer medical help in the back! I gave up the ambulance when I got married.

Superhero

When I was old enough to read my brothers' Archie comic books, I was particularly captivated by one in which Archie became a superhero by tapping into "The PH Factor." PH stands for pure heart, and he called himself, "Pureheart the Powerful." It must have been around Hallowe'en time, and I was trying to think up a costume for "trick or treating" door to door for candy.[1] I dreamed up a superhero costume and begged my mother to make it for me. She was quite the seamstress and kept us dressed nicely in the clothes she made. So I asked her to make a black cowl hood that would cover the top of my face as a mask, with a streak of lightning coming down the forehead. Then she took my red woolen pullover sweater and put a bolt of lightning on it. She added yellow stripes down each leg of a pair of black tights and a pair of green shorts over them. I'm sure I must have asked for a cape, although I don't recall what it

---

1   We did this in complete ignorance of the origins of this demonic, pagan practice.

looked like. Then I slipped into my black snow boots to finish off the outfit. I so wish I had a picture of it!

Around that same time, we kids were speaking to each other a great deal in "Pig Latin." That is a silly twist on English where you take the first letter or sound of each word and put it at the end, followed by "ay." Consequently, my name, Shary Cooper, as I was known in those days, would be Aryshay Oopercay. Now I was old enough to read, but young enough to not understand what I was reading. I didn't have a clue what a factor was in the Archie comic, but I thought it sounded good. So now that I had a superhero costume, I took it a step further beyond trick or treating. I called myself, "Aryshay Oopercay Actorfay" and decided to go have an adventure.

I donned my outfit, opened our bedroom window, and used the bunk bed ladder to climb out. Then I took our dog, Herky, for a walk. That's the part I remember. My brother, John, however, remembered that there was more to the story. Apparently Glen, the little boy down the street, was fighting with his little brother, Emory. I must have thought that the situation called for the help of a superhero, so I showed up and ordered Glen to stop fighting with his brother. Glen, however, had no respect for "Aryshay Oopercay Actorfay" or even for the costume, and punched me. I believe that was the end of the confrontation. Now John knows this story because he was hiding behind the tree watching. I can only imagine that it is likely to be true, but I successfully managed to block the unpleasant experience from my memory!

There is something in us, even as children, that wants to do the supernatural. I believe God has woven it into our DNA to be like Jesus—He made us in His image, and He is the miracle worker. He is our Model, the Pattern Son, and we have every reason to believe that when we abide in Him and He abides in us that we will do the works that He did and greater works (John 14:12).

All Types of Food

Mom loved to cook and was always trying new recipes on us. I didn't always like everything though. I remember sitting outside on the back porch one night when she served sauerkraut because I couldn't stand the smell.

She learned to eat and enjoy the food of India and had learned to cook it too—missionary strength—that is, not as hot as the locals make it. I loved the flavor, but didn't appreciate the hot spices. Dad always said that it wasn't good unless it made the perspiration stand out on your brow! My siblings had gotten accustomed to the real local food by eating with the servants, but I was just a baby when we lived there and was too young to acquire the taste. I've never been too fond of food that bites back! I don't always like everything, but have learned to eat almost anything.

When I was in high school, the first health food store came to town. I became fascinated with the subject and made a decision that has helped me enormously in life: If it's good for me, I choose to like it. Now I know that some things that are good for me taste a bit like cardboard, but I determined to like them and managed to acquire a taste for them. Later on, my ETH vows also helped me in difficult eating situations.

Born for the Nations: Canada

We lived in Howell, Michigan, about 50 miles west of Detroit. East across the Detroit River is Windsor, Ontario, Canada. We lived near enough to Canada that it was perfectly normal to have Canadian coins that we freely used as change—although they wouldn't work in vending machines! I grew up watching channel nine, CKLW, the Windsor TV channel, when the "rabbit ears" antennae were turned just right. It was a little fuzzy, but as a child I enjoyed watching The Friendly Giant on Canadian TV as much as or perhaps even more than Captain Kangaroo on American TV.

I remember getting up very early on July 1, 1969, to watch the investiture of Prince Charles when he became the Prince of Wales. I imagined, as I suppose lots of girls did, that one day I would marry him. I did find it amusing that when my own "Prince Philip" appeared in my life, our wedding day was just thirteen days before Charles and Diana had their royal event.

I also loved the Royal Canadian Mounted Police and watched the Calgary Stampede Rodeo with great delight. When the Canadian TV station went off the air for the night, I admired the beautiful maple leaf in the middle of the flag as it waved in the wind. It was deeply moving for me, but I never wondered why. I suppose that God was preparing me for the nations, and Canada was to be my first that I could remember.

The summer I was eight, when my older three siblings went off to camp, I had the privilege of going with my mother's parents to visit my uncle and aunt in Massachusetts. We had gone there on a family vacation a year or two earlier to meet the new baby cousin, David. His older brother, Neal, and I had become good friends in our earlier trip and I enjoyed the visit.

On the way home, Grandpa decided to cut across the Niagara Peninsula, crossing into Canada at Niagara Falls. I remember the border officer asking if we were all American citizens. Grandpa replied that we were and I piped up from the back seat that I had been born in India. I think Grandma was quite relieved that the officer didn't seem to have heard me! It was certainly much easier to cross the border in those days.

Baby Sister

When I returned from Massachusetts and Carole returned from church camp, Mom and Dad sat down with us to tell us the good news that Mom was expecting a baby. I blurted out,

"You're gonna have a baby? I thought you were too old for that!" She was only 38 at the time. My how our perspective changes!

When Paul and John returned from camp, Mom chose a different strategy to break the news to them. We were having ice cream for dessert after supper and Mom put pickles on hers. It wasn't long before one of the boys picked up on it and asked if she was trying to tell them something, and of course, she was.

Christina Marie Cooper was born February 12, 1967, just after a very deep snowfall. Thankfully, we were living only two blocks from the hospital, so there was no problem getting there. Chrissy was the delight of my life. I was old enough to not be jealous of the new baby of the family (that had been my position for nearly nine years), and I loved helping Mom with her.

When we moved across town to a bigger house to accommodate our larger family, we used to run out the door together every time a train would rumble through our back yard so that we could wave to the engineer.

Early Music

When we got our first piano, Mom was very happy. She would sometimes sit and play classical music or hymns. At one point Paul was taking piano lessons from a lady in town. After listening to him practice one day, I went to the piano and played the melody of the song he had been practicing. Shortly thereafter, Mom set out to give me lessons. It was always on my after school "job list" to practice for a certain amount of time, and I was to use the kitchen timer to keep myself on track. Sadly, when your mother is your teacher, it's much easier to get too busy and skip lessons. We managed to get a little ways in the process, but I never got much past beginner or intermediate.

When reading music I can play either the right hand or the left, but I find it difficult to coordinate both together.

In fourth grade, the high school band teacher, Mr. Hornyak, came to our school to give the students a musical aptitude test. Then he called in the parents of the promising ones to encourage them to get their children started in band that summer. When Mom met with him, she was expecting to have me take up the flute that Carole had tried and then put down, but he managed to talk her into getting me started on the bassoon.

We moved across town that summer and I started in another school, which had its challenges, but I loved band practice. At first we were only playing music in unison, but one day he had us play a Bach chorale, and for the first time I played the base line and the other instruments played separate parts of melody and harmony. I was thrilled! I thought I was in Heaven! Something in me was so stirred by this music in parts and I was hooked. Mr. Hornyak told us that if we would work very hard, when we got to high school, he would take us to Europe on a band tour. That made me very excited.

In sixth grade, he had me also attend the fifth grade band practice, only this time it was to learn percussion. He knew that I would need some other skill in high school band because you can't march with a bassoon. I loved that too.

However, when I got into junior high, Mr. Hornyak took another, more promising job and left me and my dreams high and dry. I didn't especially like the next couple of band directors and gave up the bassoon in ninth grade.

First Song

Grandma Parks was a member of the International Order of King's Daughters and Sons, a Christian service organization. They had a summer camp for girls near where my father grew up. At the time, Camp Missaukee appeared to me to be mostly for more privileged girls. I don't know how I was selected by my grandmother's group to be sponsored to attend the camp, but I had fun there for two weeks the summer of 1970, swimming, learning archery and doing handicrafts, etc. There were various competitions between the cabins and one evening we were supposed to sing. I don't remember much about the criteria for the competition, but I remember getting the inspiration to write new words to the tune of "This Is My Father's World." It was my first song. I think it was one of the older teenagers' cabins who won the competition, though.

Around the same time, my mother found me a guitar at a rummage sale. I was delighted—at first. It was a very cheap guitar and the strings were very high off the fretboard, so it was painful to play it for very long. It had no case and stood against the wall at the end of my bed. I diddled on it a bit and enjoyed getting some pretty sounds out of it, but I had nothing to go on to actually learn to play it. Some months later it fell over and the head broke off of it.

Meanwhile, I had also been attending Spring Hill, the church camp of the Peoples Church of Pinkney (Evangelical Free) where my family attended. It was a wonderful camp where I learned to ride horses—a typical young girl's dream. I managed to get through the beginner and intermediate courses and truly loved riding.

Filled with the Holy Spirit

My fourth grade teacher, Jean Tulip, was a Charismatic Methodist; her husband was a Methodist pastor at one time. I'm guessing that parent/teacher conferences caused my mother to become acquainted with her, and before I knew it, I was accompanying my folks to their home for Bible study. I learned how to play Rook from their sons, Billy and Charlie. As the years went by, the relationship between my parents and the Tulips continued and they continued to grow in the Lord.

The Tulips were the leaders of the Youth Department at the Michigan CFO ("Camps Farthest Out") and invited Mom and Dad to be counselors in the summer of 1971.

My little sister Chris (then age four) and I accompanied our parents to this camp that was being held on the campus of Alma College. I received the Baptism of the Holy Spirit in a big way and my mother did as well. My mother and I were deeply touched by God and so blessed at the camp. With this experience my mother and I felt a real closeness. I bought a huge cross necklace and when I wore it, Mom called me her "bishop in blue jeans." I was so on fire for God.

At the end of the camp was a baptismal service in the indoor swimming pool. So now at the age of thirteen, the opportunity to be baptized presented itself to me again. I went to my mother and told her of my desire to be baptized. She said, "Honey I think that you are old enough now to make your own decision on this. I don't think you need to talk to your dad about this one." She knew how hungry I was to make this step.

There were so many people that wanted to be baptized that four pastors lined up in the pool and baptized four at a time. I wanted very much to be baptized by one of the youth leaders, but when it came my turn, I went to someone I didn't even know. It was disappointing at first, but it turned out that the person who baptized me was the same pastor who had baptized me as a baby! He had gotten filled with the Holy Spirit and was part of that CFO Camp. Glory to God! Mrs. Tulip told me later that at the end of the baptismal service, Mom had said to her, "Jeannie, did you see the dove?" This was an indoor pool! She certainly saw something significant in the spirit!

When the camp was over, we drove up to my father's parents' farm and spent the night. I was going to Camp

Missaukee again in the area, starting that Sunday afternoon. We all went to church and the rest of the family stayed for Sunday School. Mom and I came back to do laundry so I could repack. In that short time alone together, Mom and I found each other in the Spirit as sisters in the Lord, and not just as mother and daughter. It was the most glorious moment; we had a wonderful, warm embrace and I knew there was a deeper relationship than what we had had up to that point. The experience of the Baptism in the Holy Spirit that we now shared made a beautiful, profound connection between us that had happened in the Spirit realm.

The Last Good-Bye

When my parents took to me to Camp Missaukee that afternoon, I remember Mom kissed me good-bye and said, "We'll see you in two weeks." After supper the following Thursday, Dad called the camp. It was usual for a camper to get a telephone call. The rest of campers and staff were heading out for the evening campfire, so I was left all by myself in the dining hall to talk with my dad. My dad asked if I were sitting down, so I got a chair and sat down. He said, "The Ingham County Coroner just called and your mother's body was just found in her car." There I was all alone. This was not a church camp with an evangelical emphasis, but I had one friend I knew was a Christian who was a counselor—and it was her day off! I was all alone with the Holy Spirit, my new Friend, the Comforter. And He SHOWED UP! I felt so embraced by Him; so protected and cared for. I wandered around the camp, going back to my cabin, but no one was there. I went to look for my friend and she was not there. Finally I went to the director and told her what had happened. She called for the nurse to get me a sedative, but I told them that I didn't need one. I was full of the peace of God, and they were falling apart! Arrangements were made to get me home, along with my sister, Carole, who was on staff at another camp not far away.

Mom had been trying for years to lose weight so that we could go back to the mission field. I had some trouble with obesity when I was a child as well. I weighed 104 lbs. as a third grader (that's eight years of age!). The summer I was twelve Mom and I went on Weight Watchers diet together for mutual moral support. I managed to lose some weight at about the same time I had a growth spurt and reached a more "normal" size. I just hated it when Mom would buy me clothes in "Chubby" sizes!

For some years Mom went to a doctor that specialized in weight loss. He administered diet pills and diuretics, but apparently failed to prescribe potassium supplements. The autopsy was inconclusive for the cause of her death, but we have surmised that it was probably due to an electrolyte imbalance. A car pulled out in front of her and she swerved to avoid a collision, but evidently the shock was greater than her imbalanced electrolytes could handle and her heart stopped.

We know that she had never been in a higher place in God than she was following her receiving the Baptism in the Holy Spirit. She had suffered some depression as a result of being denied permission to return to India in earlier years. Dad said that having Chris was such blessing to her soul, to take care of a new baby. But now she was so full of the joy of the Lord at the CFO Camp that she testified about how the Lord had lifted all the worry off of her. My eldest brother, Paul, had enlisted in the Navy (it was the Viet Nam war era), and Mom was deeply concerned for him. She said, "He's been stationed on a submarine—and of all things, he's steering the thing!" The peace of the Lord became real to her as she gave Paul's safety into the Lord's care.

The Lord chose to take her Home to be with Him from the very highest pinnacle of her spiritual experience. He knows what He's doing and I've learned to trust Him more deeply as a result.

The death of my mother without a doubt changed my life and had profound impact on all my family. We had some very intensely hard times but the Holy Spirit was so good to meet the need and to keep us.

The first Christmas without Mom, my grandparents bought me a guitar. This one had nylon strings and was easier on my fingers. I bought a chord book and a book of Christian songs that showed the chords with the music. Within a few days I was playing and singing. It came to me so easily! I'm convinced that God gives gifts to us because we will need them as the tools for the calling He has placed on our lives. I believe that every musician has the calling of a worshipper on them. If they haven't found the Lord yet, they just don't realize Whom they were designed to worship!

Stepmother

My father married Virginia Eldred Cooper when I was fifteen and there were some serious complications in the situation. I was not pleased to have a stepmother. I'm sure that stepmothers know how complicated this is. For the stepchild, it is just as complicated when someone else tries to step in to take the place of a parent. A stepparent may have the best of intentions, but without divine intervention, it is very difficult for a child to accept a stepparent, unless the child is very young.

Virginia had three teen-aged children: Daryl and Loren, who fit between John and Carole in age, and Marcia, who was between Carole and me. I just could not accept my stepmother and after a few months of trying to live in the same house with a "blended family," I went to live with my mother's parents for the last two and a half years of high school. I had a great deal of bitterness in my heart toward her and carried it for many years.

My stepmother knew Robert Doorn from church when they were youngsters in Grand Rapids. The Doorns moved to Brighton, a town nearby, and they began a church called Christian Fellowship Center (CFC). I met them one evening when I popped in at my dad's to collect some belongings, and they just happened to be visiting with their their baby, Susan.

With Grandma and Grandpa Parks

Living with Grandma and Grandpa Parks was a blessing. I needed them and I think they also needed me. We were good for each other. Grandma had arthritis and Parkinson's disease and was glad for my help around the house.

The summer I turned 16, as soon as I got my driver's permit, we started out on a trip to Massachusetts. I accumulated a lot of miles of driving experience in a short time. I think that was also preparation for the many, many miles of travel I would do as an adult.

High School

I enjoyed High School, for the most part. Due to overcrowding, our school was on a "swing shift" with the upper classmen coming in early and the freshmen coming only in the afternoon. As a sophomore (tenth grade), I arrived midmorning and took some classes with the juniors and seniors, then I held over to take some classes with the younger ones. My favorite classes were—well, just about everything but math!

My first class of the day was A Capella Choir. When I arrived in class the first day, I learned that there was a requirement to audition to get into it. It was also hay fever season and I was

31

struggling with allergies. Rod Bushey, the choir teacher, arranged a time for me to sing for him. I was worried that I might have to change classes, but after the audition, I was pleasantly surprised that I had not only made it into the A Capella Choir, but also the Highlander Chorale which was a select group out of the A Capella Choir. The Chorale group did harder music and had the privilege of singing in more extracurricular activities. I loved singing in the two groups. Mr. Bushey was a wonderful teacher, and was also the minister of music at the local Nazarene Church. We had multiple concerts each year. He always had a sacred concert as well and I am grateful to this day for all the scripture that I learned through the sacred music.

As a junior, I took Music Theory and loved it. We were analyzing Bach chorales and how they were "constructed." Our final assignment was to write a chorale and orchestrate it for the band. I was one of those kids that put off assignments until the last possible time. I was up all night finishing the orchestrating and got sick, so I couldn't hear the band play it.

By that time I was reasonably proficient on the guitar and had written a number of songs. Sometimes people would ask me to sing, and I sang in the local talent shows.

I believe it was during that time that I decided to go on to college and study music. That summer I attended a choir camp at Western Michigan University. I rejoined the band in order to get as much experience in music as I could. School starts with marching season for football, so I was given a glockenspiel (bells designed for marching) and wasn't coordinated enough to play them and march at the same time. Then I was given a bass drum and did well—it wasn't too complicated!

When concert season came again, I took up the bassoon. The only time I was ever first chair was when I was the only bassoonist. If there were two, I was second chair. If there were three, I was third chair, and yes, at one time there were four of us and I sat fourth chair. I think it was mostly because I was lazy and didn't work very hard at it.

By this time, I was pretty independent and just wanted to do my own thing. I completely forgot about being a missionary. I wanted to be a music teacher, unless, of course, I was "discovered" and became a recording artist.

The Bible Smugglers

In April of my senior year in high school, Grandma and Grandpa decided to take a vacation and visit relatives in California. They also planned to tour around Arizona. They asked Carole and her husband, Mark, to stay with me while they were gone. Carole and Mark were very burdened for me and had been praying for me intently.

About six months earlier, Carole had invited me to come to Christian Fellowship Center to hear these ladies that smuggled Bibles behind the Iron Curtain. They were known as "Gwen and Sigi." I thought that was pretty interesting, so I went to CFC to hear them. Sister Gwen sang and played her accordion, and I was touched by the music. Then Sigi preached and all I could do was cry. I didn't even know why I was crying. When she finished her message, I thought that if I just sat there and cried, maybe they would lay hands on me and prophesy over me to help me understand why I was crying. All I knew was there was something about these women that had something to do with me!

While my grandparents were on vacation, Carole invited me out to lunch for my 18th birthday. She took me to a ladies luncheon that Sister Doorn was sponsoring in conjunction with their Easter Convention, and Sister Gwen was the speaker. Once again I was deeply moved, but this time while Sister Gwen was speaking, I heard a voice in my spirit say, *"I want you: I want you one hundred percent, and I want you right now!"*

I did not know of any reason to argue, nor did I want to disagree in any way, so I just said, "Yes."

I attended another meeting or two during that Convention. I was captivated by the stories that Sister Gwen told about our suffering brothers and sisters behind the Iron Curtain. The stories of risking their lives to smuggle Bibles resonated in my spirit. One evening after the service ended, I asked Sister Gwen if I could minister to her by massaging her shoulders. She agreed and Brother Doorn showed us a room to the side of the platform where we could go. As I rubbed her shoulders, she told me how much she appreciated my gift to her, and said, "If I am ever arrested, imprisoned and beaten, I will remember this massage and it will bring me comfort."

I said to her, "If that ever happens, I want to be there with you." In my heart I wanted to become a Bible smuggler and work behind the Iron Curtain bringing comfort to our persecuted brethren there.

The Lord used that encounter to reawaken my love for Him so much that I wanted to attend CFC every time the doors opened, and I sat on "Glory Row." That's right up front where the hungry ones sit.

However, when I got back to my usual activities of home, school, and choir, etc. I started to mull over my situation. I reasoned, "I am already enrolled at the music school at Western Michigan, so I will go ahead and go for a year." I had some scholarships and my grandparents were encouraging me to go, so why not?

When Sister Gwen had been at CFC in April, she announced the End-Time Handmaidens First World Convention was to be held in Dogpatch, Arkansas over Memorial Day weekend at the end of May. The Doorns were taking a group of people to it and

Carole and Mark and I wanted to go. So off we went, and we all stayed in one of the rental chalets together in the area of the convention center.

Before the meetings even started, I went into the convention center and walked around and prayed. There were a few flags of the nations where Sister Gwen had been, hung up around the balcony. Once the convention started, I could always be found sitting in the front row, right in the center, "eating up" everything that was going on. I was so hungry for God; I just wanted anything and everything that God had.

One afternoon in between meetings, Carole and Mark and a few of us decided to try and find Engeltal.[2] We drove to the place where we understood it was and looked over the valley from the side of the highway. There was a cloud hiding it from view. On the way back to the convention center we stopped at a souvenir shop. I wasn't interested in souvenirs, so I wandered around outside the shop. The view was so magnificent! I remember saying to myself, "I could live here."

Back in the meetings, every speaker was wonderfully anointed, and I found myself being so gloriously filled with the Presence of the Lord. It was in one of those meetings that Brother Doorn stepped up and said, "I feel that we are supposed to lay hands on those who feel that they are called to be End-Time Handmaidens. If you feel you are an End-Time Handmaiden, come up to the front and Sister Gwen will lead you in a prayer." I was out of my seat in a flash. Many of us lined up to have some of the ministers lay hands on us, and Sister Gwen led us in the prayer that became the vows of the End-Time Handmaidens:

> Lord, I give myself to You;
> I give my life to You.
> I want to be your End-Time Handmaiden;
> I feel Your call;

2   Engeltal is a German word that means "Valley of Angels." It is the location of the End-Time Handmaidens, Inc. headquarters.

I believe I was sent
To do the will of my Father.
I will take orders from You.
I will submit to You.
I will let You break my will.
I will not seek for comfort
Nor high position,
Nor to do what I want to do.
Mine is the humblest task,
Or the most dangerous task;
By the grace of God I will do it.
I will sleep where You want me to sleep,
I will eat what You give me to eat,
And when I have nothing, I will not complain.
If I go to prison I will rejoice.
And I will praise You
Because You've been to prison for me.
I love You, Jesus;
I thank You for calling me,
And that You want me,
And that You can use me;
And all I can say is,
"Send the Fire
and burn up the sacrifice.
Fill me with Thy Holy Spirit
And give me a double portion
of Thine anointing."

Amen

"You Will Take Her Place
When She Is Gone"

During one of those meetings while Sister Gwen was speaking, I heard that same Voice in my spirit that I had heard a month earlier say, "YOU WILL TAKE HER PLACE WHEN SHE

TAKE THE LID OFF

This was the last photo of Mom that we know of. It was taken in the Peoples Church of Pinckney.

On Dad and Virginia's wedding day..

Loren, me, John, Carole, Paul, Marcia, Daryl,

Dad, Chris, Virginia

Sister Gwen had just led us in the ETH&S Vows for the first time, and called us up to have the ministers lay hands on us.

That's me below her in the foreground with the braid on the back of my head.

IS GONE" and I fell on my knees and I wept. At some point in that convention, I knew that if I went to college I would never serve God.

When I had an opportunity, I said to Sister Gwen, "I believe the Lord wants me to come and work with you." At another time I even said to her, "You are Elijah and I'm Elisha." I probably scared her!

Later she told me, "Honey, I don't think this is the time for you to come to Engeltal."

I returned home from the convention and told Grandma and Grandpa about my decision to serve God and not go to college. Grandma went digging in Mom's old letters and came up with this one:

May 7, 1947

My dearest family,

I hope you are all together when you read this letter, because I have something very important to tell you. This is the most important decision I have ever made. It's this: I'm going to the mission field in Europe. During Bible Conference, Peter Deyneka told about his recent trip to Europe. He told how people would walk fifteen or twenty miles to attend a Gospel meeting, stand up for four or five hours of service, and then wouldn't let him close because they were so anxious to hear about salvation. Right then I knew that that was where I have to go. I've got something those people haven't got, and it's not fair to keep it to myself. I never realized before what conditions those countries are in. They are eager to hear the Gospel of Christ, and if they don't get it, they'll drift into atheism. I feel tremendously inadequate and useless, but I know that with God leading me, I can do anything through Him.

I want to be thoroughly prepared. I'm changing my major in the University from piano to Christian missions with a minor in Russian. And wherever the Lord leads me, I'll go.

I hope you'll be praying for me and stand back of me in this, because it means giving up all I've planned, but I'm willing to do it, because Christ gave up all He had for me.

Love, Elaine

Grandma's motive was to show me how Mom had changed her major, but continued to go to college to prepare herself for missionary work. I only saw that my mother hadn't ever fulfilled her call. I felt that the burden was now mine to bear.

It was two weeks before my High School graduation. I wrote to the college and told them I will not be attending and they could give my scholarships to somebody else. I went to my high school counselor and told him the same thing.

A month or two later, I learned that these End-Time Handmaidens were going to be in Ontario, only a few hours' drive from my home. Arrangements were made for me to drive there with one of Sister Gwen's nieces. The event was being held at Shalom, a farm that had been turned into a retreat center. Sister Gwen began teaching about the Tribes of Israel[3] and how, since we as Gentiles have been grafted into the root of Israel, we each have a place in one of the tribes. I was fascinated. During that event, I had my first experience of the Holy Spirit moving on me in a kind of prayer that feels rather like you are birthing a baby in the spirit realm. I didn't understand it at the time, but Sister Gwen explained to me that it was travailing intercessory prayer.[4]

---

3   See Engeltalpress.com or call (870) 446-2665 to order.
4   See Gwen Shaw's book *Pour Out Your Heart* on Engeltalpress.com

Shalom was the same place that Sister Gwen and Papa Jim had their wedding in 1972. They celebrated their fourth anniversary during this event and brought out the last bit of the wedding cake to share with us. Sister Gwen brought a plate with a few tiny bite-sized pieces of that lovely fruit cake to the girls dorm room in which we were staying. As she offered it to us, she said, "May you all be married within one year!"

The farm house had plenty of rooms for sleeping, but only one bathroom, if I recall correctly. Early one morning I was on my way there and discovered Sister Gwen in line ahead of me. She was wearing her bathrobe and hadn't yet put up her hair. I remarked, "Wow! Your hair is so long!"

She explained to me that there are nations where the culture requires women to have long hair, so she kept her hair long to be able to minister in those nations. The thought made a lot of sense to me, and since I already had long hair at that point, I have kept it long ever since. Of course, I am listening to the Lord for His input about my appearance. I have fond memories of brushing Sister Gwen's long hair for her through the years—it was always the best time to have a heart-to-heart chat.

Language School

I took a summer job working as a "sorter" at the local Salvation Army Salvage Store. That means that it was my privilege to sort through the used clothing that was donated and decide what was saleable and what should be made into rags. The bags and boxes that were brought to us had often sat in basements, attics, or garages from the time the clothes were removed from a person's belongings before they ever made it to the donation bin at the store. In the meantime, the clothes acquired smells, vermin and—well, what the vermin left behind. It was not a pleasant job! During those weeks, I cluelessly waited on God for direction.

Brother Marcos Dermendyieff, "Mr. Argentina," had been at the World Convention, and Carole and Mark had been quite captivated by the Lord regarding him. They felt that the Lord wanted them to go to Argentina and work with Brother Marcos.

They found out about King's Way Missionary Institute, a place where Spirit-filled people can go and learn Spanish for the purpose of going to the mission field. So they signed up to go. I did not know what else to do, so I told my sister that if they would accept me on this short notice, I would take that from God and go. Sure enough they accepted me and then I wished I had some scholarships, but it was too late—I had given them away. I went by faith and God provided for schooling. I did not really want to be there; I wanted to be smuggling bibles behind the Iron Curtain. That was where my heart was; I wanted to be learning Russian or German. I had taken German in high school during my senior year. But Spanish—why Spanish?

I wrote Sister Gwen my question and her reply was: "The Lord spoke to me and said, 'If you want a piece of the harvest, look to the Spanish-speaking nations.' If you really want to smuggle Bibles, you can smuggle Bibles to Cuba, it is both Spanish and Communist." She encouraged me along those lines to go ahead and finish my Spanish schooling. Even though I did not understand this leading, I followed through with it. It was during my time in language school that I did my first 21-day fast. I was amazed at the grace of God that came with it that I could manage to study while fasting.

A few months before I graduated, I contacted Engeltal and said, "I would like to come and help for the summer and see what else God might have planned for me."

The person that answered the phone said, "I don't know, I don't think so, because there are going to be so many people here after convention that there will not be enough room for you."

I was stunned—I really thought I had heard from God on this one. So I let it go and went on to the next thing. There was a young man at the school that played the piano, guitar and banjo (I always fell for musicians!). He invited me to attend the school banquet with him. When he brought me back to the girls' dormitory, we sat in the truck for a long time just chatting. He shared with me his list of criteria for a wife: she was to be tall, with long hair, and she had to be able to sing!

I thought, "Surely that must be me!" And I remembered that Sister Gwen had wished for us to be married when we shared the last of her wedding cake. So when he asked me to marry him, I agreed. That engagement lasted about two weeks—God got through to me in short order that this was not His plan. One of the things God used to tip me off that I was missing it was that the people I knew and trusted in the spirit didn't react very well when I told them about the engagement. So now I always tell young people to pay attention to the opinions of the people they trust in the spirit when they are choosing a mate.

When I broke it off with him, he was heartbroken, but was able to find the right one within the next six months.

One of the requirements at Kingsway was to attend services in Spanish at least once a week, and before long we were required to stand up and recite a scripture in Spanish. By the second semester, we had to stand and give a testimony. It was very good experience. I went across the border many times during my stay at Kingsway and a couple of times since. I learned to love Mexico.

I managed to graduate as the valedictorian of the class, but I'm not so sure that it was such a great accomplishment since the whole class was in the top ten! I highly recommend this school to anyone who has a calling to the Spanish-speaking peoples of the world. It is excellent!

Engeltal

Once school was out, I still did not know what I was supposed to do for the summer. But I knew that I knew, that I knew I was supposed be in Dogpatch for the End-Time Handmaidens Second World Convention. I bought a one way ticket because I did not know where I was to go from there.

I had made some tentative plans with my roommate from language school, to visit her home in South Carolina; maybe we would go to Mexico and do something for the summer.

I got to the World Convention and the same person that said "there will not be a place for you," said to me, "Sharon, I'm so glad you're here! Would you like to be the head usher?"

"Sure, what do I do?"

So she told me to water the plants, help people find their seats and help with the collection when it was time.

"Ok," I agreed, "I think I can handle that." I diligently watered the plants every day, helped with seating people and taking up the offerings.

Part way through the convention, Sister Gwen came to me and said, "Sharon, the girls are expecting you to come to Engeltal after the convention."

"I'm not planning to. I had no idea," I responded.

"Oh well," she replied, "Just pray about it."

The next day the same person who said that I could not come, put her arm around me and said "Sharon, I really think you're supposed to come to Engeltal after the convention."

"Really?" I said. "Out of the mouth of two or three witnesses let everything be established—I guess I'll come." That is how I came to Engeltal.

Myrna Kogele was also at that convention and had been at the previous one too. The two of us went to Engeltal in her red pick-up truck. But I was not very content because I had had other plans, so it "upset my apple cart" to come there now. It's as though I had forgotten my desire from the previous convention.

"We'll Make Sharon the Cook"

The next morning I was coming up towards the kitchen in Sister Gwen's house, and I overheard her talking with another gal. Sister Gwen said, "We'll make Sharon the cook." I sat down hard on the nearest piece of furniture! I could cook enough for myself to get by. That is how I got through language school. My knowledge of cooking was pretty limited and there were twelve people to cook for! I knew how to open a can of corned beef hash and put the contents in a corning ware dish, break an egg on top of it, and bake it. I had learned how do that, but that is not exactly the kind of cooking they were looking for! My mother had died before she could teach me very much in the way of kitchen skills.

Sometimes the staff ladies would find me backed up against the cupboards in the kitchen just wringing my hands, wondering what to do next. I didn't know what to do! Sister Gwen was gracious and so were the other girls; they would help me get started and taught me some basics.

Sister Gwen showed me how to make rice in a big heavy pot. She said, "You put in enough rice to cover your first knuckle, then you add water up to your second knuckle. Then you put the lid on, turn up the heat, and don't take it off until the rice is done."

"How do you know when that is?" I asked.

"You just have to know by the Spirit!" she replied, chuckling.

I was unsettled in my soul because I hadn't planned to come to Engeltal after being rejected months earlier. It was as if I had erased it from my mind as an option. That, coupled with the nerve-wracking job of cooking when I didn't know how, gave me a troubled countenance.

After a few weeks, Sister Gwen called me to her room and said with concern, "Sharon, I can see that you are not happy here. There is a lady here from Michigan and she is leaving tomorrow. You can ride back to Michigan with her, or if you want to wait a few more days Papa Jim and I are flying up to Michigan and we can take you."

All I could do was cry, I did not know what to do, and I did not know what to think. She saw me crying and not responding, so she said, "You just go back to your room and pray about it and come back and see me later."

So I went to my room and cried and prayed some more, but I didn't receive any answers. When I returned to her room I just sat there and cried. Sister Gwen prayed for me and then she said, "The Lord shows me that you don't have a home to go back to" I burst into more tears, because it was true.

By this time my grandparents, with whom I had lived in Michigan, had moved to Arizona. I had left my father and step-mother's home and my heart had not been healed from that issue yet, so I did not want to go back there. Sister Gwen said, "You can stay. Maybe what you need is another 21-day fast."

So I fasted again. This time on hot lemon and honey drinks. In that fast God put my roots down into Engeltal. He made me excited about being the cook. I started reading recipe books, getting all energized about cooking. "I can do this," I thought, with no more wringing of my hands in the corner. Here I was trying to cook without even tasting the food! Through the years I've noticed that the food is always better when the cook is fasting. It must be the anointing!

I had an appointment with my grandparents to drive them from Arizona to Michigan to celebrate their 50th Wedding Anniversary. I arrived in Arizona the last day of my fast. I learned the hard way how not to break a fast. I thought that since I had gone without calories for all these days, I could eat whatever I wanted without being concerned. I had lost fifteen pounds on the fast and I gained back thirty! The point is that you need to be careful coming off of a fast. Once you put that weight on, it is really hard to lose. Your body goes into starvation mode and when it sees food, and just grabs every morsel and saves it for the next time it might be starved. Years later I learned a better way to come off a fast—take as many days to go back to normal eating as the number of days you fasted. It takes longer for your body to regain any weight that you lost without taking on too much weight.

In those days that I was visiting Michigan, all I could think was that I want to come home to Engeltal. The Lord had done a work of grace in me during that fast that made me feel Engeltal was my home. Not long after I returned, the Lord brought another young lady to Engeltal and she was given the position of cook. I had overcome my "trial by fire," actually learning to enjoy cooking, and apparently the Lord had finished the work in me that He was after. I moved on to work in the office, first checking names and addresses on the mailing list, and later answering letters. I remember one of the Handmaidens shocked expression when we met. I had been writing to her in response to her pleas for prayer. She hadn't expected me to be so young.

That first summer, I was also given the job of picking blackberries so one of the ladies could turn them into jam. Day after day I picked blackberries—when I closed my eyes to pray, all I saw was blackberries!

It seems that the chiggers and ticks are always looking for fresh blood. They seem to have a sense about it when someone new arrives in the area. Or maybe it's just that when you've have scores, or maybe hundreds of bites at one time, you learn where not to walk! That first summer was certainly an itchy one!

Sometimes I was given a task I didn't know how to do. Natalia would always say, "You're an End-Time Handmaiden—you can do anything!"

Sister Gwen had an expression in Chinese that she always used when we were stumped about how to do something: *Shiang egeh bangfa*. It literally means, make a way or think up a method. She used the expression frequently and it became my method of operating. Consequently, I don't give up easily on a project. If I run up against a difficulty, I just try to get creative and think up a way to make it work. Of course, I have to thank the Holy Spirit for inspiration.

Poplar Bluff

Before she came to Engeltal, Myrna had taught school in Poplar Bluff, Missouri for Pastor Louise Copeland, the President of International Ministers Forum. When Myrna's mother came from Montana to visit her, she also wanted to see the place Myrna had been the year before, so several of us went there for a visit.

I liked Sister Copeland, and because I was so unsettled in Engeltal, I told her, "If you ever need any help, just let me know. I'll be glad to come." She didn't need help at the time, but some months later she did. She called Sister Gwen and asked for me to come and help in her school. It had transitioned into an ACE school, so it didn't require a teaching degree like Myrna had when she taught there.

By this time I had fasted and felt so very settled with my roots deep into Engeltal and I didn't want to go to Poplar Bluff, but Sister Gwen felt that it was the Lord's will for a season. I'm grateful for what I learned there, but I was so glad to get back to my home in Engeltal!

Third World Convention

The Third World Convention (1978) was my first one as a staff member. I was assigned the delightful task of teaching the children. I diligently prepared lessons using Sister Gwen's book, *Sigi and I*, telling the stories and having the coloring book that Sister Gwen's son Tommy illustrated for them to colour. I truly enjoyed myself and believe that good seeds were sown into good ground. Some relationships formed then have endured through the years.

Israel

Grandma and Grandpa had set aside a trust fund for me, expecting me to use it for my education. After I had been at Engeltal for a year, the annual Israel Tour was on the horizon. I called Grandma and Grandpa to ask if I might use the funds in the account to pay for the trip. After some discussion that made my intention clear about having given up my plans for a college education, they agreed that travel was also educational and gave their permission. While the group was forming, I assisted with the correspondence, and once the trip began, I was called upon to assist with the details of keeping everything running smoothly. Little did I know (or anyone else for that matter) that I was being prepared to coordinate the Israel tours after that.

Year after year I was privileged to go with the group to help Sister Gwen and Papa Jim, and each year I kept on learning more. It soon became my passion to help people experience the "Land of our Spiritual Forefathers." It's one thing to read a book and then see it acted out in a "Technicolor" movie, but it's even greater to read "The Book" and walk on the very Land it describes, going for a boat ride on the one and only Sea of

Galilee in the World and walk on the Temple Mount where the first and second Temples of the Lord God of Israel stood. Something happens that builds your faith in the reality and absolute truth of the Bible when you lift your eyes to view the mountains of Moab where Ruth came from and paddle around in the Dead Sea (without sinking), imagining where the stone structures of Sodom and Gomorrah might have been reduced to ash by fire and brimstone falling from the sky. The Jordan River is such a quiet stream, now that modern farming employs irrigation. Walking on the streets of Jaffa/Joppa makes you think back to the cranky prophet Jonah trying to flee from God's orders to preach to a people he didn't want to see spared, and then remember that the Holy Spirit first fell on the Gentiles in the house of Cornelius.

It is always thrilling to me to watch the dawning of revelation on people's faces as the Bible comes alive to them and their own spiritual walk deepens in the knowledge of proof positive right before their eyes of Bible not only being true, but being the best guidebook available for touring this Land.[5]

Argentina

In January of 1978, Sigi and David Oblander were planning a trip to Argentina with their toddler daughter, Tammy. I was asked to go along to help take care of the little one and help out with simple interpreting since I could speak a little Spanish. We went to a number of places around the country. When we arrived in Mar Del Plata, I enjoyed seeing my sister Carole and her husband Mark and their toddler son, Nathanael. They had come to help Brother Marcos with his orphanage.

Sigi ministered at a pastor's conference in Bahía Blanca. It was a wonderful conference and many appreciated Sigi's ministry. She always had a vibrant word.

---

5   Be sure to check our website for the next tour that we will be taking. www.endtimehandmaidens.org

The experience that impacted me the most on that trip was meeting people to whom Sister Gwen had ministered prophetically twelve years earlier and hearing their stories of how everything she prophesied had come to pass. Their lives had been transformed by God under her ministry. What a track record!

The Publications Department

I began working in the publications process when I was given the job of proofreading *Love, the Law of the Angels*[6] when Sister Gwen compiled it in a few days' time from tapes of messages she had preached in Germany.

Then when she wrote *Day by Day*,[7] I had the privilege of proofreading it. My proofreading skills have improved over the years. I don't think I did a very good job with either of those books, although we have noticed that it doesn't seem to matter how many people we have proofreading, no one finds all the errors, and several people on a project can all completely miss at least a few.

Dedication Song

About a week or so before our Fourth World Convention in 1979, we were working late into the night in the office when Papa Jim walked in and said, "Why don't you take the rest of the afternoon off?" We chuckled and closed up for the night. At that time the office was in the basement of Sister Gwen and Papa Jim's house and to get to our rooms we had to walk up seven stairs and through the "Red Room" (so named because of the colour of the carpet) where the grand piano was. Sister Gwen couldn't resist sitting down to play, although it was

---

6   To order, see engeltalpress.com or call (870) 446-2665.
7   See engeltalpress.com or call (870) 446-2665 to order.

probably around two in the morning. Once she started playing, the rest of us couldn't resist the pleasure of staying with her to sing along while she played. I was reading the music over her shoulder as she played one song after another. Then she began playing something that wasn't written on the music in front of her. To me it sounded like a grand coronation march.

Then Liesel Mueller stepped up and said the first line: "We come to serve our Lord and King." So we sang it together. Then I sang the second line: "And raise up high His banner." I'll never forget the look of joy on Sister Gwen's face as she sang: "Our lives we gladly, gladly bring" and Liesel sang, "To serve and love Him ever." We sang it through a few times and retired for bed.

The next morning, Sister Gwen came downstairs from her room with the next verse:

> We dedicate our lives to Him
> To live for Him forever
> For He has saved us from our sin,
> And He'll forsake us never.

At some point during the day, I received the third verse:

> Then we shall go to meet our King
> When this earthly life is over.
> We'll gather 'round His throne and sing
> His praise forever and ever.

We were thrilled to have received a new song from the Lord and quickly typed it up to include it in the little pink sheet that we added to our chorus book.

When the Convention time came, one of our speakers, Fritz Söhlke from Germany, a Bible Smuggler, was telling about his experiences behind the Iron Curtain. He told a story about a young Russian Christian woman who required surgery to remove her voice box due to disease. Before she was put under the anaesthetic, the Communist doctor told her she wouldn't be able to speak when she awoke from the surgery and asked her if she had any last words. She replied that she did and recited a poem. At this point, Brother Söhlke pulled a small, pink piece of paper from his pocket and began to read:

> "We come to serve our Lord and King
> And raise up high His banner.
> Our lives we gladly, gladly bring
> To serve and love Him ever…"

Sister Gwen shouted, "That's our song! That's our song!" Brother Söhlke had found it in our chorus sheet and thought that Sister Gwen had gotten it in Russia and translated it into English! How amazing are the works of the Lord! He loves to astound us with His wonders!

Christian Booksellers Association

When I first came to Engeltal, our book department consisted of about seven books by Sister Gwen, and about five by other authors. She continued writing and we continued printing as the years went by. Around this time, Cliff Dudley of New Leaf Press suggested to Sister Gwen that she ought to promote our books at the Christian Booksellers Association Convention, and he helped us get started. We went there annually for many years. It was Cliff that suggested that we give a name to the publishing arm of the ministry, as it seemed that people were turned off by the name End-Time Handmaidens. He suggested Engeltal Press, and it stuck.

Our first time to attend the Booksellers convention, it was held in St. Louis. During that event, someone suggested to Sister Gwen that St. Louis was a very good place for us to hold our World Convention, since air connections to get to Dogpatch were limited and expensive.

A Middle-of-the-Night Concert

Sister Gwen and Papa Jim had Myrna and me come along to assist with the selling of our books that first time. We were very frugal, so the four of us shared a room. In the middle of the night, Myrna and I both woke up to the rumbling of a thunderous concert of snoring coming from the other bed. We tried telling them that they were snoring. We tried asking them to roll over. We tried everything we could think of—but to no avail! I don't know how long we lay awake being disturbed, but eventually fell asleep from sheer exhaustion. We didn't get much sleep that time.

The next time I had to share a room with them, I knew what I was in for, so I prayed and asked the Lord to help me. I decided in the depths of my spirit that I really wanted to be there with them, so I would consider any kind of noise would simply be music to my ears. And it worked! Although I heard the snoring, it never bothered me again! Hallelujah!

A Love Slave

On one of our trips to Israel, Sister Gwen and Papa Jim were having dinner with Ruth Heflin. I was going table-to-table making announcements to the tour members. When I stopped by their table, we chatted for a few minutes. Sister Ruth asked me "What is it like at Engeltal? I hear that you're a slave when you go there."

I laughed and said, "Of course it's true! I'm a love slave!"

Exodus 21 gives the laws concerning Hebrew servants. They could only be kept for six years and then they were to be set free. But if the master gave the man a wife who was also a servant, when his time to be set free would come, he could decide, because of his love for his master, his wife, and his children, to remain a slave for the rest of his life.

53

I loved Sister Gwen and Papa Jim, and I loved the work of the ministry. I was happy and content. There was nothing in the world that appealed to me to make me want to leave or pursue any other career or lifestyle.

The Print Shop

The Lord brought a wife (Linda) and daughter (Aimee) for our printer, Karl Ubrig. When their son came along, he began to feel a stirring in his soul to return to his native land of Germany. Now the question was, "Who will do the printing?" Sister Gwen was burdened, and we were all praying about it. I began to feel a burden to take it on, so I went to Sister Gwen to volunteer. She got out her bottle of oil and anointed me to learn. Karl trained me for two weeks and left for Chicago to try and earn some money for their trip. When he returned, he taught me a few more tricks of the trade and moved to Germany with his family.

I remember before he left the first time that he had mostly focused on the smaller Multilith machine. At one point I was struggling terribly with the Multi and decided to try to run the bigger ATF Chief. Even though I had only watched Karl run it and hadn't had any hands on practice, I was able to get the job done successfully. I guess it was a case of shiang egeh bangfa! Another time I was running the Chief and it wasn't running properly. I prayed and asked the Lord to show me how to fix the problem. The next thing I knew, I found that my hands were making adjustments that I didn't know existed, and the job ran just fine from that point on, glory to His Name!

Prince Philip

It's more fun to tell this story with the help of my husband, Philip. I hope you will enjoy it this way.

Philip: I was born and raised on Chicago's South Side, and then we moved out to the suburbs in 1967. Sister Gwen would come to Chicago when she was on furlough, because her brother had a church there. My family and I went to that church and my mom became Sister Gwen's best friend. I backslid during my teenage years when I got some independence. You know—the car, high school, friends—I never got into drugs or alcohol or anything like that—I was just backslidden.

Sister Gwen would come to the house unannounced sometimes. I would have the headphones on just rocking out, and she would walk in the front door. I would wave hi and she would wave and as soon as she would turn her back, I would just shut everything off and be out the door. Once I was going out the door and found she had blocked my car in, so I got my bike out of the basement and took off. I would not come home until that car was gone! Sometimes it would be there for a long time. I was afraid she had a prophetic word, and it was not what I wanted to hear. I was always being dragged off to meetings; I think the only drug problem I had was being "drug" to meetings! We would go up on the North Side, and we'd go into the Puerto Rican churches and the Black churches. I just always tried to sit on the back row.

In 1974 I was so backslidden and tired of hearing about the end times, that when I started getting interested in a worldly girl, I took advantage of the opportunity to get out of the house and married her.

Sister Gwen moved to Arkansas at the end of that year and Mom and Dad followed her there in 1975. They found a house on the opposite side of the mountain from Engeltal. I was left up in Chicago alone, except for my Mom's sister, Nancy, and her family, and Grandma Cain was living with them.

I had a dream in 1976 that I was sitting next to Colonel Jim, and I had headphones on with this recording equipment in front of me. I was sitting at a table next to the stage and all these people were out there in front of me. When I woke up, I thought, "That is the craziest thing I ever dreamed in my life!"

The worldly marriage ended in divorce, and I decided to change my job from working in a steel company to construction—bad move! It wasn't for me. Then I tried working as a glazer, installing windows. Later I got a job offer to work in a chemical plant that would pay more and was closer to home. It was a "no-brainer" to me to take the job. Then in 1980 the recession was raging and things were just bad; everything was going downhill and the chemical company had their first layoff in one hundred years—and I had only been working there for seven months, so I was among the first to be laid off.

There were times when I was about to get in my car and drive out to see friends on the North Side and the thought would hit me, "If you die out there, do you know where you are going?" So I would not go; I would not leave, and I think God had saved me from something there.

The last thing to go was my bowling average. I used to love to bowl and played on three leagues. But when God has a plan for your life, He will just take things away from you and you know it.

I was working part time as an assistant manager of the bowling alley, and when things got slow I would just shoot frame after frame trying to figure out why my game was so off. When God is going to mess you up, He is just going to mess you up!

Sharon: Sister Gwen used to say, "If God is fixin' to fix you, you'd better let Him fix you, or He'll fix another fix to fix you!"

Philip: I had already been down to Dallas that summer to visit my brother, Scott. The unemployment there was three and a half percent, compared with over eleven percent in Chicago. Scott and his wife Carolyn were with a fellowship there and no one in the fellowship was out of a job. They said, "If it is God's will for you to be here, you will have a job. I was in Dallas one day and I thought, "This is not for me."

On the way back to Chicago, I stopped to visit Mom and Dad. When I found out that Sister Gwen was away, I went to Engeltal with Dad to fish in the pond. I had had a copy of Sigi's life story and had loaned it to a guy in the bowling alley, since he thought that there was nothing wrong with Communism. He never gave it back, so I stopped in to buy another copy of the book. I met Sharon in the office, and we chatted for a few minutes.

Sharon: I remember enjoying a friendly chat with Philip. As I watched him go out the door, I thought, "He's a nice guy— what a nice guy!"

Philip: In December I got a letter in the mail from the unemployment office. I had been faithfully looking for work, and I thought I had one year of unemployment benefits that would give me three more months of living expense money to find work, but the letter said I only had two weeks left and no more. I was living in a two-bedroom apartment by myself and no means of support. My aunt and uncle on the north side of the city suggested I go and visit my family for Christmas, "Go see your mom and dad, and we will help you go."

So I went to visit Mom and Dad. On Christmas Eve at 10:30 p.m., they were getting ready to go out the door, so I asked where they were going. They said, "To Engeltal, we have some gifts for the girls. Do you want to come with?"

By this time I was 26 years old and I had run from Sister Gwen all those years. I thought, "It is Christmas Eve and its 10:30 at night. There won't be any Holy Roller prayer meeting going on. I will be all right, and I might as well face the music sometime." So off we went. As we arrived, Sharon answered the door and most of the staff was just leaving. They had had their Christmas together and the party was over. Sister Gwen encouraged Sharon to stay and sing this new Christmas song the Lord had given her. She sang the song and then Mom says, "Philip plays the guitar."

Sister Gwen said, "Sharon, why don't you go get your guitar and let Phil play for us." I was just learning classical guitar at that time. Sharon brought her guitar, and so I played the bits and pieces of things I could remember since I didn't have my music with me. I was playing this nice Spanish piece, when Sharon says, "That's beautiful! What do you call it?"

I cleared my throat and said, "Romance." I found out later it had a different name.

Sharon: About that time, the phone rang. It was one of the gals I was going out the door with, when Sister Gwen grabbed me to come back and sing. It was my friend, Myrna. She said, "Sharon, where are you? What are you doing?"

I said, "Philip is playing guitar for us."

She replied, "Uh-oh! Daa da da daaaa. Daa da da daaaa," singing the "Here Comes the Bride" theme.

I said, "Myrna, come on!"

She said, "No, this is it. This is the one!"

Philip: So as the time moved on, Sharon and I were talking in the dining room while Mom and Sister Gwen were in the kitchen talking and sharing too.

Sharon: We were just chatting. I was so impressed with the fact that he was not trying to impress me. He was just chatting and being nice. We had been talking about classical music and classical guitar. I had these albums of hymns on the classical guitar, and was telling him about them and how much he would enjoy them.

When they left, Sister Gwen and I sat in the living room for a long time. She told me all about Philip, because she had known him for some years. She told me how he loved mice and snakes and had all these little animals. She shared a lot of stories about him. While we were just sitting there chatting, the phone rang again (by this time, it was midnight) and it was Philip's mother, Dorothy Buss. Sister Gwen took the call up in her room. She came back and said that Dorothy would like to invite any of the girls to come for Christmas Dinner—maybe Sharon would like to come. I was so naive I did not even see it coming!

Dorothy had left her gloves behind, so I thought, "Okay, I can take Dorothy her gloves, and I can take the albums for Philip to hear. I'm sure he will like them." So I agreed to go. Christmas Day came and none of the other girls wanted to go! So I went up the mountain with the albums in my hand, but I forgot the gloves. I guess I had something else on my mind.

We were all sitting at the table, and I looked around: there is Philip and his mom and dad, Grandma Cain, his brother, Gary, and Gary's wife Kristine, their two children and me. I suddenly realized, "this is a family gathering!" I really felt out of place.

When dinner was over, it was time to open presents—and they had presents under the Christmas tree for me! Talk about moving fast—Busses can be fast!

Then it was time to sing around the piano. Dorothy was a tremendous pianist and violinist. She sat down at the piano and "just happened" to have these pieces of music for quartets handy. Gary is a bass, Philip is a tenor, I'm an alto, and Kristine is a soprano. We were singing this beautiful quartet music and Kristine says, "Wow! We sound terrific! We could be a group— what shall we call ourselves?"

In my heart I said, "Kristine if you will just be quiet for a little while, maybe we can call ourselves the Busses," because by then I was beginning to get it.

Philip: I ended up staying an extra week with my parents in Arkansas, even having New Years dinner at Engeltal, but I still was not saved; I was still a backslider. I had such a peace

59

because I knew this was where I was supposed to be. When I went back to Chicago, I started a 21-day fast, and on the fourth day of my fast I realized I need to get saved! So right there in my living room, I knelt to ask the Lord to forgive my sins and I gave my life back to Him. My lease was up at the end of January, so in that one month's time I wrapped my whole life up in Chicago. I drove my car down and rented a truck with my dad, and brought all my stuff to Arkansas.

When we got back and unloaded my stuff at my parents' house, I had four days of my fast left. I thought, "I have not really spent a lot of time with the Lord. I feel I need to fast an extra week." and My flesh did not really want to fast 28 days, but I just felt I had to do this.

Some people said, "You don't have to do that, 21 days is enough. Don't be ridiculous!"

Sharon said, "Just do what you feel the Lord wants you to do." So I fasted this extra week not knowing why. Two weeks later, we went to a regional convention in Georgia. In the afternoon meeting, I took my vows and joined the End-Time Handmaidens and Servants.

Sharon: We had been sitting together during these meetings. After Philip got up and told his testimony, he came back and sat next to me. Sister Gwen went up to the pulpit and said, "Sharon has been teaching Philip how to print. And I don't know what all has been going on in that print shop, but something tells me we'd better hurry up and get the chapel finished!" We were so embarrassed and sat there like a couple of tomatoes, all red in the face.

Philip: So in the meeting that night, I got filled with the Holy Ghost. When I got up off the floor, I staggered over to Sharon, really drunk on the new wine. I said to her, "How would you like to get engaged?" I would have never done that in my right mind at that time. We had only gone on one date!

60

Sharon: I thought I would play that line a little longer. I wanted to make the moment last as long as possible! So I said, "Engaged for what?"

Then he said, "To get married!"

Of course I said, "Yes!"

After the meeting we told Sister Gwen about our engagement and asked her when we could set the date for the wedding, as we wanted her to perform the ceremony. She said, "We are going to be home in July. How would you like to be married on July 17? That's Jim's and my anniversary." We readily agreed. That was a sweet, sweet, delight to be able to share anniversaries with them. Every year we would have our special anniversary dinners together.

I had only been in charge of the print shop since shortly before Christmas, so it was only a matter of weeks before Philip was on the scene. So I taught Philip everything I knew about printing, and being very mechanically inclined, he took right to it and went way beyond my abilities. I still did the darkroom photography, developed the negatives, and then made plates for him to put on the presses.

Philip: The World Convention was the first week of July, and I was assigned to help Papa Jim. I was sitting next to him at a table full of recording equipment, next to the stage. It was the only time they ever had the recording booth next to the stage. I had the headphones on and I looked at all this gear, and I looked at all those people. Then the dream came back to me from five years earlier. I had completely forgotten about it. Wow, since that dream I had had three different jobs. I couldn't have orchestrated those events!

So about one week and a half after the World Convention we got married on Friday, July 17, 1981. Early Sunday morning, we joined Sister Gwen and Papa Jim at the local

61

airport to fly with them in their plane to California to have a "working honeymoon" at the Christian Booksellers Convention. We were also able to go to Disneyland and went swimming in the Pacific Ocean at Long Beach.

Sharon: The rest of the story? Before Philip showed up in my life, I knew it was just about time for "Mr. Right" to come along, so I had put my radar on. I was looking, and looking. "Is it him? Or is it him? I was already the Israel Tour Coordinator by that time, and that year the tour group had some very nice young men on it. There was one in particular that struck my interest and he happened to strike the interest of one of the other girls on the staff. Somehow she made it clear that he was off limits to me. So I said in my heart, "Lord, if he is the one for me let him fast 21 days to be an End-Time Servant and an extra seven for me." Papa Jim had fasted 28 days before the Lord gave Sister Gwen to him, so I thought that would make a good "fleece."[8]

Well that young man didn't do it, but this young man, Philip, did! So we were set up! It was a God set-up! I feel like we have an "arranged marriage." It was totally arranged by God—and of course, Sister Gwen and Dorothy helped! I had a great deal of confidence also from the fact that everyone I trusted in the spirit approved.

God knows what he is doing in our lives, and He has this divine set-up for us! You can count on Him to do a divine set-up for you, if you will just TRUST HIM! IT IS ALL ABOUT TRUST.

---

8   Putting out a "fleece" refers to the story of Gideon in the Bible. God called him to fight the Midianites and Amalekites, but he wasn't so sure about it, so he put a fleece of wool on the ground and asked God to confirm the word to him by letting the dew fall only on the fleece and not on the ground. Next morning, the ground was dry and when he wrung out the fleece, there was so much water that it filled a bowl. He still wasn't sure, so he put out the fleece again and asked God to confirm His word by letting the ground be wet with the dew, but asked that the fleece be dry. That is what happened, so Gideon knew he should obey the orders he had received from God.

TAKE THE LID OFF

Natalia, Naphtali, Sister Gwen, and me at the Third World Convention in Dogpatch

Tammy, Sister Gwen and me
Can you believe the hair?!

On duty with the Newton County Volunteer Ambulance Service

The night of our engagement in Douglas, Georgia

Philip: Papa Jim was a retired Lt. Colonel from the Air Force. He just had an air about him; he was a colonel, military, very regimented, and strong. That was Papa Jim—he was just an incredible man. A man came to him once and said, "What is it like to be in a women's ministry and your wife is the president? You're the man!" He said, "I spent 28 years in the service. I know rank, and my wife's got it!"

I feel the same way. I have been involved in the ministry with Sister Gwen for 32 years now. I know rank when I see it, and Sharon's got it!

Our Wedding Songs:

When we planned our wedding, we each wrote a song for the other and didn't sing them to each other until the wedding. Here are the lyrics:

I Was Born for You

I was born for you;
You were born for me.
God had planned our lives
From before eternity.
He made you to be my husband
And me to be your wife,
For you fulfil the things
That are missing in my life.
And I fulfil in you
The things you're missing too.

We were two separate halves
Only half able to live,
Only half able to serve
And only half able to give.
But God knew our need
And reaching down from above

TAKE THE LID OFF

He put the two of us together
And held us there with love
And now in Him we are one
And we've only just begun.

Day after day the two of us will grow
The more we come to be like Him,
The more His love will show.

— Sharon Cooper Buss

Song of Love to You

My love I sing to you this day,
God has surely shown us the way,
Your face, it shines just like the sun,
You are truly God's chosen one,
You are truly God's chosen one.

Your soul is flowing with God's love,
Your eyes are shining like stars above
Your love so strong I truly know,
God has joined us to be one,
God has joined us to be one.

Arise my love with me this day,
Our love is bonded here today,
God will guide us through the land,
In the nations we will stand,
In the nations we will stand

Chorus:
Hallelujah, to Christ, the King,
He has shown us the way,
Following His perfect will,
He's with us this day,
He's with us this day.

TAKE THE LID OFF

Hallelujah, Glory to His name,
Hallelujah, Praise be to God this day,
Praise be to God this day.

—Philip James Buss

We also sang together "The Wedding Prayer" that our friend, Ramona Dicks, had written for the wedding of someone in her family. It so fit the thoughts of our hearts, that we wanted to include it in our ceremony.

Wedding Prayer

Lord, as we stand here before you,
Send Your blessing from above.
Lord You have brought us together,
Please now join our hearts in love.

Chorus:
For we are Thine,
Together we are Thine.
We will be kind and tender every day.
Unfailing love covers and forgives.
We come to You and seek Your perfect way.

Lord we want our lives to shine
So that men will see only You
Come, Lord, we want You to lead us:
What we say and think and do. (Chorus)

Lyrics and Music by Ramona D. Dicks, BMI

Throughout the years of our marriage, if I got a little out of sorts with Philip, he would just sing to me a line from this song, "We will be kind and tender every day." That usually straightened me up in short order.

TAKE THE LID OFF

At the Sixth World Convention in 1981 at the St. Louis Airport Marriott Hotel, just two weeks before our wedding

Singing "The Wedding Prayer" by Ramona Dicks at our wedding.

Papa Jim and Sister Gwen blessing us with their cups of punch

Philip's First Israel Tour

The annual Israel Tour that year was very special. Sister Gwen had it in her heart to go "from Dan to Beersheba" and we actually went even farther than Beersheba to Eilat and saw King Solomon's Copper Mines along the way. We saw the crater in Ramon. It was just before the Sinai Peninsula was to be given back the control of Egypt, so we made it a point to tour the area while it was still possible. We went on a boat ride on the Red Sea to view the beautiful coral and colorful fish. It was a very unusual tour.

We were so blessed that Philip was able to go along this time. The Lord provided his way by discovering that his Grandma Buss had purchased some US Savings Bonds for him when he was a baby. Now, twenty-six years later, they were worth enough to pay his way. Seeing sights we hadn't seen before or since, and getting to share it with my husband as newlyweds was really wonderful. We had a beautiful ceremony on the shores of the Sea of Galilee to bless the marriages of all the couples in the group. The next morning we awoke to the most beautiful sunrise. I jumped out of bed and grabbed my camera. The photo I snapped that morning became the cover of Sister Gwen's best-selling devotional book, Day by Day.

Rainbow House of Prayer

In 1950, Ed and Bessie Bergman, Sister Gwen's parents, decided it was better to live on the New York side of the Niagara River so Ed wouldn't have to commute every day across the Rainbow Bridge to his factory job. The big, old boarding house at 222 6th Street became their home and they made it a place of warm welcome, especially to the saints of God. Bessie would always come from the kitchen with good food as Ed welcomed their guests at the door. They always held special meetings when missionaries would come to town.

TAKE THE LID OFF

We call this a
"Double-Decker Buss"

Gary's children,
Angela and Joel,
and Philip's dad, Estel
are looking on.

Philip's first camel ride

Standing on the Temple Mount with
the Mount of Olives in the background

Just chillin'

Sister Gwen and her family always made this place their home when they were on furlough from the mission field. Sometimes they lived in the attic when all the rooms were rented. One time when she came to visit, she felt the Lord spoke to her from the scripture, 1 Kings 17:14, "...The barrel of meal shall not waste, neither shall the cruse of oil fail, until the day that the LORD sendeth rain upon the earth." She felt this was the Lord's promise that there would always be provision there. Another time she saw a huge angel standing near the stairs and knew that the Lord would always keep the place safe.

When Jesus came and took Ed home in 1972, Bessie (better known as "Mom" Bergman) stayed on and continued the hospitality, hosting "Prayer and Praise" meetings along with End-Time Handmaiden and Servant Dora and Hank Horbinski. The house was filled with intercession and worship, lifting the mighty name of Jesus in praise.

Then Mom began to consider selling the house and eventually moved to Arkansas without having been able to sell it. Mom said, "Gwen, why don't you buy it? I think the Lord wants you to have it." But Sister Gwen felt she had her hands full just running Engeltal, the End-Time Handmaidens and Servants Headquarters, and didn't want to take her mother's advice. As time passed and no one bought the house, the Lord spoke to Sister Gwen and said, "There's not enough money in Niagara Falls to buy that house, because I want you to have it." Finally she said, "Lord, if you'll give me the whole amount in one cheque, I'll know it's Your will." Within weeks the one cheque was on her desk and she bought out her brothers' portions of the inheritance and the dedication of Rainbow House to the Lord came to a new level! Renovations and remodeling began and just a few months later the first Rainbow House Retreat was held in the Fall of 1983. Philip and I had the "privilege," along with Jill Lilley and Myrna, to don our "grubbies" and clean the attic to make room for some of us to sleep there during the retreat. The roof had been going bad and the tar paper had disintegrated. We were black by the time we finished the job!

The Lord gave the vision for Rainbow House of Prayer to be:

Rainbow House of Prayer

• An extension of Engeltal.

• A place for Bible study, prayer, praise and worship.

• A place for retreats, for people to get away from the "normal" and get into the Presence of God and enjoy the wonder of His creation at Niagara Falls.

• A place of launching for ministry into Canada. The Rainbow Bridge that connects the United States with Canada is only seven blocks away.

In the succeeding years, the Lord enabled End-Time Handmaidens and Servants to purchase the lots surrounding Rainbow House, which included a two-bedroom cottage.

More Nations: India

In 1983, we went with Sister Gwen on a ministry tour to India. Many of the contacts that she had worked with through her many years of ministering there invited her to come again, bringing a group. It was a tremendous experience. We went to New Delhi, Faridabad, Jaipur, Agra, Benares (Varanasi), Hyderabad, Madras (Chennai), Calcutta (Kolkata), Bombay (Mumbai), and even took a side trip to Kathmandu, Nepal. It was a ministry marathon!

Philip and I took our guitars with us and it was really the first time that we began to sing together on a regular basis and lead praise and worship. Many lives were touched as Sister Gwen preached and the team prayed for the precious souls of India.

It was my first time back to India since I had left as an infant. I was moved by all the sights and sounds and smells. I was moved by the precious souls bowing to idols, and my heart cried out for them—this veritable sea of humanity being swept down the raging current of idolatry and darkness. We took a boat ride on the Ganges River at Benares (known today as Varanasi), and watched the people burning their dead, hoping to help them improve their station in their "next life." It was disconcerting to see young Americans and Europeans who were there searching for truth and only finding fascinating imitations. I could see why hearts that long to serve Jesus could easily be called to lay down their lives for Him there.

Our End-Time Handmaiden, Joyce Scott and her husband, Bill, hosted us in Madras. She came from America and he from Ireland to be missionaries to India. They were in charge of the India Bible League at one time and did lots of printing of Bibles, tracts, and teaching materials in the many languages of this nation of diverse people groups. We were impressed with the magnitude of the work.

One of the meetings we had in Calcutta was in a Chinese church. There were both Mandarin and Cantonese speakers, so Sister Gwen would preach in English, then it was interpreted into each language. It got to be hard plowing, so Sister Gwen apologized to the tour group and began preaching in Mandarin to save the time and the anointing.

The burden for India is still with me. I have returned twice to India since then, mostly to minister among our End-Time Handmaidens and Servants in the Himalayas. They are so inspiring!

72

England and Scotland

When the tour group went home to the USA, Philip and I accompanied Sister Gwen and Papa Jim on their journey to England and Scotland. Francine Rocco (at the time, now Lovell) had arranged wonderful meetings in London before we drove to Blackpool, England, for the British Christian Booksellers Convention. There we met some of the family of Eric Liddel, the Olympic runner whose story is presented in the movie, Chariots of Fire. Sister Gwen had been so inspired by the story and the theme music by Vangelis that she wrote these words to sing to that tune:

Verse 1
I hear Your call, Lord, and I will run
To the uttermost nations to tell of Your Son;
I'll pay the price, Lord, no matter how great.
I know You'll go with me till I reach Heaven's gate.

CHORUS:
No mountain too high to climb for You.
No valley too deep
To keep me from bringing love to those
Who never have heard.
Nothing in this world can hold me back
From giving my all.
I give you the best that I can,
For I've heard Your call.

Verse 2
Thy Kingdom come, Lord, Thy will be done
On earth as in Heaven, Through Jesus, Your Son.
I'll run a straight race, Lord, Till I reach the goal.
Your Spirit within me will strengthen my soul.
© 1982 End-Time Handmaidens

Singing that song always stirs my heart to run the race for the Lord with My eyes on Him as my goal.

From Blackpool, we drove up to Scotland. Francine had arranged meetings in the Camerons' church in Peterhead. What glory meetings they were! These people knew and loved revival and the Holy Spirit was pleased to come and provide it. In the middle of Sister Gwen's preaching, a powerhouse Scottish evangelist named Jackie Richey came charging up the aisle from the back of the church, prophesying that God would use Sister Gwen in the great end-time revival in Scotland. My heart immediately leaped and resonated with those words. "I want to be there and be a part of it too," I prayed.

Papa Jim wanted to trace his ancestors who had come from Thurso, the northernmost tip of the mainland, so we drove up there. We stood in the gale force winds in John O'Groates, another northernmost place, and realized we had to lean into the wind to be able to stand up.

On the way back from Thurso, we were going down very narrow roads on top of steep inclines with stone walls on either side. There was a truck coming toward us and suddenly, another truck pulled out to pass the first one. The road was so narrow that you couldn't really consider it two lanes, so Papa Jim was forced to pull off the road. Thankfully, at that precise place, the stone wall was replaced by a hedge, so the damage wasn't as bad as it might have been. I was in the back seat reading and Philip was beside me, watching the scenario unfold. He reached up to grab the seat in front of him to brace for the impact, and he felt and heard a snap in his collar bone. When we got out of the car, he couldn't move his right arm. We prayed much for him for the Lord to touch and heal him.

Eventually we made it to the nearest hospital, which was in Glasgow, and had it x-rayed. The doctor told him that it appeared that it had been broken, but was now mended. That night we were playing our guitars together in the church in Peterhead, rejoicing in the goodness and greatness of our God!

The Orient

In 1984, Sister Gwen and Papa Jim lead a small group that consisted of Jim and Francine Lovell, Ernestine Shelton, June Lewis, Philip and me, to some of the nations of the Orient. We landed in Taiwan and had a Holy Ghost outpouring in Taipei and Kaohsiung. Then we flew to Singapore for meetings arranged by Brother Goh Ewe Kung. He was a camera dealer and presented the ministry with a 35mm camera with a 28-300mm lens. It was a beauty! And I was allowed to use it. I had always had an interest in photography and this got me fully committed!

Then we went to Indonesia to hold powerful meetings in churches from the Gereja Isa Almasih denomination. We went all over the island of Java from Jakarta to Bandung (at a Bible school) to Surabaya to Malang. What a beautiful, green country it is with its rice fields, smoking volcanoes, tropical fruits, and beautiful people! Sister Gwen told us that if we wanted to come back to Indonesia, we needed to learn to like durian, a really stinky fruit that tastes a bit like turpentine custard. I loved this place, so I ate the stuff each time it was offered to me. I needed to eat it just a few more times, I think, in order to cultivate a liking for it. I chose to "like" it so I could come back, but still didn't find it pleasant.

Brother Tan Kee Hian, son of Grandma Tan that Sister Gwen tells about,[9] welcomed us to his church in Malang. He also took us to a camp in the mountains that was run by his ministry. I preached to the young people there and God moved on their hearts. And his son, a photographer, taught me how to

---

9 Grandma Tan was a Buddhist and died of heart trouble. When the family and Buddhist priest came for her "encoffining" ceremony, a Bible Woman showed up and prayed for her to be raised from the dead. Everyone was astonished when Grandma Tan opened her eyes and sat up. She pointed to the family idol shelf and said, "Get rid of all that stuff. This family is going to serve the Lord Jesus Christ! I just met Him and He sent me back."

Standing by the North Sea with Jane Strachen, Francine Rocco Lovell, Sister Gwen, and Philip

Bread and cheese for lunch on the hood of the car

Our booth at the British Christian Booksellers Association in Blackpool, England

Singing in Singapore

Preaching at Christian Retreat in Bradenton, Florida

use that new camera when he took Philip and me out for a ride in the country.

Then we went to Hong Kong to round out our trip. It was getting close to Christmas and the decorations and lights on the buildings were stunning. We enjoyed high tea at the Peninsula Hotel for a marvelous cultural experience. The string ensemble in the balcony played Christmas music while we sipped our tea.

Argentina

A team of at least twelve was assembled to go to Argentina the following year. We went many places and saw many lives changed by God as the Holy Spirit moved in a mighty way. Churches in the areas of Buenos Aires, Mar del Plata, Mendoza, Salta, Esquel, and Rio Gallegos received a move of God as members of our team went there.

When we went to the south to Rio Gallegos, for days I had been hearing in my spirit, "Rio Turbio. Rio Turbio." Philip and I had been scheduled to go from there with Sister Gwen and Papa Jim to Ushuaia, the southernmost city in the world, but something came up that caused Brother Marcos, our main interpreter and organizer of the trip, to ask me to consider going to Rio Turbio. Of course I agreed and went with a small team there and on to Puerto Natales, Chile nearby.

The trip was hard—165 miles on gravel roads. The drivers took it at a much faster pace than what we would consider safe, and every time we hit a bump, the dust would puff out from behind the back seat of the car as though propelled by a bellows. Philip had it even worse in a pickup truck. Marta, the wife of my driver, who pastored the church in Chile, told us that by the time we arrived, we would be able to grow potatoes in our hair!

When we arrived in Rio Turbio, we met our hostess, Hermana (Sister) Candelaria. She was totally delighted to see me. She said, "We met at a pastors meeting in Bahía Blanca years ago, and I prayed that the Lord would send you here!" Our interpreter for those meetings had a very strong American accent and wasn't exceptionally skilled at interpreting. When it came my turn to preach, I decided to try and do it in Spanish. It was a stretch, but good experience. The Lord moved in a marvelous way—He's so wonderful!

In Salta, the Holy Spirit was so powerful. It was such a privilege to pray for the people and watch how their strength simply went out of them and they melted in the mighty Presence of the Lord. He did a powerful work in their lives as they lay on the floor, undergoing spiritual surgery by the Great Physician.

Europe

Sometimes on our Israel tours we would fly via European cities and have an overnight stopover and tour. One year we added a Convention in Zurich, hosted by Edwin and Margaret Farner. Oh how we loved the Swiss and their beautiful country. The Alps are such spectacular mountains with beautiful lakes besides.

USA

All this time we also travelled with Sister Gwen and Papa Jim in the United States. Sometimes our trips lasted for weeks at a time. Sometimes we travelled on the "Aglow" circuits and many lives were transformed by the power of God. A few of those ladies resonated with Sister Gwen's ministry and became End-Time Handmaidens. Later we began having regional conventions in different places around the country: Chicago, Kansas City, Tulsa, Columbus, Detroit, Coalinga, Billings, Minneapolis, Grand Forks, Washington, DC, Jacksonville, FL, Nashua, NH. We also travelled with her when she went to minister at Blue Mountain Christian Retreat in Pennsylvania every year in the spring.

Philip and I were the "roadies." Sometimes a team would also come from Engeltal to the ones that were closer to home, but much of the time it was just the two of us. We'd roll into a place and hang flags, set up the books and tape duplication equipment. Then we'd dress up for the meetings and lead the praise and worship. When the meeting was over, we'd sing and play for the duration of the altar service, typically thirty to forty-five minutes. Then we'd go to the back and duplicate the tapes of the messages and type up the labels for them. Thankfully, some of the local End-Time Handmaidens and Servants would help to run the book table. When everyone left, we would go to our room, grab a snack and count the offering and book sales. If it was a weekend regional, we'd finish Saturday night, pack up all the books, flags and other equipment, and sleep a very little. Early in the morning we would check out of the hotel and head for a church service where Sister Gwen would preach. The next day we'd pile in the van and head for the next place. Whew! One time at the end of a series of Conventions, Philip said, "We've burned the candle at both ends so much that there's no wax left in the middle." He was concerned about getting around any prophetic people that might pick up on his tired out attitude. Actually, though, he remained patient and kind through the many miles and meetings. I'm so grateful to God for him. He's still such a nice guy!

Philip has always been an amazing long-distance driver. I used to be good at it before I married him, but he spoiled me! We often would drive through the night to get to places. It was partly to save money on lodging, and partly because it was always so hard to get the loose ends tied up before leaving Engeltal. It seemed that if we were just going for a day trip, we'd be late leaving by an hour. If we were going for a weekend, it would be three to five hours, but if we were going to be gone for a week or more, we'd often lose a half a day or more.

When we were going to Coalinga, California for a regional that Ruth Long had set up, Philip drove nearly the whole way. I think I drove perhaps an hour or two of it. We decided that we should take the opportunity to take a side trip to the Grand Canyon. It was about an hour's drive out of the way. It was November and there were no tourists in sight. As we were leaving the park, we nearly got caught in an ice storm. We were glad we had taken the side trip, as we've never passed through that way again with the time to be able to go. Once we got back on our planned journey and crossed into California, we realized that we still had a lot of hours of driving before we would reach Coalinga. The whole trip was 43 hours! I can't tell you how much coffee Philip drank to go that distance, but he sure "crashed" when we arrived!

Sometimes Philip would drive the van, and I would fly with Sister Gwen and Papa Jim in their little plane. Papa Jim would put me in the co-pilot's seat and Sister Gwen would sit in the back and write or read. He was a marvelous teacher, and I learned how to hold a heading and altitude. He even let me take off once. I was hoping to learn more and would have loved to become a pilot, but he had a heart attack that grounded him, and we sold the plane.

I Forgive You

During one of our regional conventions in Tulsa, Sister Gwen was preaching and the anointing was high, as usual. Then she shifted the direction of the message and began to preach about forgiveness. I groaned inwardly, because I knew that I still had a bitter root in my heart toward my stepmother. Many times conviction had come over me and many times I had prayed, but I never could get complete victory in my heart.

As she closed her message, Sister Gwen challenged us to "make an altar before God" right at our seats. I dropped to my knees feeling like, "Here we go again," not really expecting anything to change.

Sister Gwen went around the room praying for different ones. When she got to me, she laid her hand on my head and prayed, "Lord, help Sharon to forgive. She didn't know what she was doing."

In a flash, the revelation hit me—she didn't know what she was doing to me? Then all of a sudden, it was as though a tidal wave of the grace to forgive washed over me and I was free. Before I left the meeting that night, the Lord gave me a song that expressed my heart.

I Forgive You

For years I searched and struggled
To find some way to forgive.
I tried and tried to release the hurts,
Do that I could freely live.
But the best I could get was eighty percent;
The wound wasn't still quite healed.
But now God's grace has come within
And to His healing hand I yield.

Chorus:
I forgive you. I forgive you
Just as Jesus has forgiven me.
I forgive you. I forgive you
Just as Jesus has forgiven me.

All those years I was blinded
By unforgiveness within.
Perhaps I was trying to fool myself,
But I knew that unforgiveness is sin.
And sin works death within the soul
And darkness to the eyes.
But Jesus has given me His light
So I can recognize those lies.

81

2nd Chorus
Please forgive me. Please forgive me
Just as Jesus has forgiven you.
Please forgive me. Please forgive me
Just as Jesus has forgiven you.

Tag
I forgive you, please forgive me
Just as Jesus—let us forgive.

From that time on, my relationship was different with my stepmother, thanks be to God!

Publishing

When we were back at Engeltal from our travels, I was in charge of the publishing of books, and printing Sister Gwen's "Angel Letters,"[10] Magazines, and tracts. She was an amazing visionary, and we would *shiang egeh bangfa* to get things done when it often seemed impossible in the amount of time we had. I suppose that at times the publishing would also be the reason we would be running late when trying to leave on a trip.

As the printing ministry grew, we had a team of as many as five working in the print shop. In the early days of our publishing, the typesetting was done by Jenny Ellingson, and her husband Don typeset the music. Eventually, we bought the typesetter from her and began doing it in-house. When Sister

---

10 Before I arrived at Engeltal, an Auto-Typist machine was installed. It operates much like a player piano and can be programmed to type a form letter. Sister Gwen would compose her news letter and Papa Jim would punch the paper roll so the machine would type each letter individually. Then we would add personal answers to correspondence. When Sister Gwen saw it work for the first time, she exclaimed, "It's just like an angel is typing it for us!" That's how the news letters came to be known as "Angel Letters." We acquired three more machines like this that I learned how to program. The correspondence eventually became more than we could handle and we began to print the news part and answer personally at the bottom.

Gwen would write a new book, we would do the whole thing if it was a book that could be bound by saddle stitching (staples in the spine). Someone encouraged us to get her books "perfect bound" (glued with a square spine), and a few of them were done by a printing company.

Sister Gwen and Papa Jim had lived through the Great Depression and were very frugal. So did my parents, and my Dutch blood and upbringing gave me the same mindset for being tight with spending. So when it came to the printing, we thought that we could do it all ourselves and it would cost the ministry less money. For a while we printed the text part of the book and jobbed out the covers. Then we would collate the books ourselves and take them to a bindery in Missouri. The next step was to get our own binder, and eventually we even bought a huge press so that we could print our own covers.

When it was time to print the magazine, in the early days, Jenny typeset it in long columns and I would do the cutting and pasting (I mean by hand—that's where the expression comes from that we use on computers now) for the page layout, then we'd shoot negatives, strip them onto masking sheets and burn plates. Philip would take the plates and print the pages, then fold them on the folding machine. Then we'd gather everyone and have a collating party, and go 'round and around the tables in our dining room. Then one or two people would staple the spines and box them up. Then we'd load them into the van and take them to St. Louis to be labeled. We even helped with that process, and the folks at Mission Center International would take them to the post office.

Every innovation we could *shiang egeh bangfa* would help us do it more ourselves. For instance, we found semi-automatic collating machines that allowed us to collate faster with flat sheets, so the extra manpower just had to fold the magazines by hand before stapling.

83

Stretch Limitlessly

One year in the 1980's, the word of the Lord came one morning during our devotions. The Lord was calling us to stretch. So I set my heart to stretch; we had some amazing workloads at that time. Sometimes I was so tired that I didn't think I could go any further. Once I saw myself as fabric that had been stretched so much that you could see through the fibers of the cloth like as if it were cheesecloth. Then I called out to the Lord for help to stretch, and had a vision of angels with something like paint rollers on a long pole. They were rolling a rubbery substance on the threads to give more ability to stretch.

That particular year, immediately after the World Convention (which is exhausting in itself), we had to head straight out to Atlanta to the Christian Booksellers Convention. The World Convention has an anointing that carries you through it, but there isn't much anointing at the Booksellers Convention. So again, I set my heart to stretch and flew through both events with the grace of God. Unfortunately, my mindset for stretching hadn't gone beyond these two events. Somehow I had it in my head that once we got back to Engeltal, the pressure would somehow let up. It didn't. And I reached my end point. I went whining to Sister Gwen, "I don't think I can stretch anymore!"

She looked at me with her flashing, prophetic eyes, pointed her prophetic finger at me and said, "You can stretch limitlessly, if you keep your spirit right!"

The message hit me like a fire, penetrating into my spirit. It was sealed in me—and it has stood me in good stead many, many times through the years.

A Daughter from the Lord

After five years of marriage and about three years of travelling with Sister Gwen and Papa Jim, Mary Ellen Rawls, our bookstore manager, encouraged me to pray about having a baby. When Philip and I visited my sister, Carole, and her family, we saw their prayer list on their refrigerator. Along with other prayer requests was written, prayer for Aunt Sharon and Uncle Phil to have a baby. It seemed that God may have had something on His agenda, and my heart began to get lined up with it.

Following our annual New Year's Eve prayer time to usher in the year 1987, Philip and I asked Sister Gwen and Papa Jim if they would pray with us about having a baby.

Some months earlier, Sister Gwen had written her powerful Bible study, Redeeming the Land.[11] During the first few months of 1987, we took a day to redeem the land around Engeltal, breaking the curses and restoring God's blessing on the land. One of the blessings that is promised in Deuteronomy 28 is that you will be fruitful.

In April, after our regional convention in Minneapolis, I realized we were expecting. We had to return to Engeltal for a few days to get packed up for the next series of regionals, so I took the opportunity to break the news to the staff. We were served ice cream for dessert one night after supper, so I followed Mom's example and put pickles on top of my serving. After much longer than I thought it would take, someone at the other end of the table said, "If I didn't know better, I'd think you were trying to tell us something!"

To which I replied, "I am!!" and the place erupted in joy! Around the same time, one of the other young couples in Engeltal announced that they were also expecting. We walked together every day for exercise. Her labor was induced and the doctor declared that the baby was about three weeks early. Heather was born three weeks later. Redeeming the land had resulted in a blessing of fruitfulness!

---

11 Order from engeltalpress.com or call (870) 446-2665.

France

I was about five months along in my pregnancy when Philip and I went to France to redeem the land with Rona Spiropoulos, our leader, Leann Gilespie, Joan O'Connor, Lisa Sutterby, and our interpreter, Diana Ehrensperger. Sister Gwen was scheduled to speak in Panassac at the camp meeting hosted by Sergine and André Snanoudj, near Toulouse. We flew into Brussels, Belgium, and rented a VW van (it was cheaper there than in Paris) to drive to the south of France. It was the beginning of August and we quickly learned that all of France had closed up shop and gone on vacation. The traffic at times was bumper to bumber and came to a virtual standstill when the traffic light in the next town miles away turned red.

Impact Camp in Panassac was truly a camp out in the country. The meetings were held in a large tent and we slept in tents also. At first Philip and I stayed in a two-man pup tent. I could hardly maneuver to get dressed in that confined space, due to my abnormal center of gravity. We moved into the bigger tent with the other girls and managed much better for the duration. At times the girls enjoyed watching the baby kick me as we lay on our sleeping bags in the tent. We sang and testified in the meetings and had a wonderful time watching God at work in people's lives.

After the camp meeting was over, we headed north to redeem the land and hand out tracts in the streets as we went. Along the way, Philip and I decided to stay in the van when the other girls went out to hand out tracts at a beach where the ladies were bathing topless.

We went to Le Mans, home of the famous racing tour. Then we redeemed in Rouen, where Joan of Arc was burned at the stake. My how we interceded there! We went to Dieppe where the rain and gale winds whipped us mercilessly as we redeemed and prayed for God to forgive the terrible bloodshed that had taken place there. One thousand Canadian troops were killed and another two thousand were taken prisoner in that place during World War II.

From there we went to St. Mer Iglise and the five beaches of Normandy, where so many lives were lost in the D-Day invasion on June 6, 1944. As we finished praying on the last beach, the sunset painted the sky with glorious gold. We danced in the waters of the English Channel as the tide came in. We knew that we had the victory.

Our final city was Caen. We first went to the town's pedestrian mall to sing in the streets and hand out tracts. Hardly anyone even looked our way. There was simply no response and tracts we handed out were thrown on the ground. We decided that we had better change our strategy and went to the castle of William the Conqueror. It was late afternoon and the place would soon be closing, so we had to get guidance rapidly from the Lord for what He wanted us to do. As we walked around spreading the Holy Communion elements as we went, I had a vision of soldiers in chain mail armor with swords and spears coming toward us. The Holy Spirit came over me, and I began to laugh heartily. I couldn't stop laughing. The more I laughed, the more demoralized these soldiers became. They stopped their advance, lowered their weapons, then turned and slunk away. It only made me laugh all the more. How wonderful the Lord's strategy was that day. When we finished, we went back to the pedestrian mall to sing and hand out tracts. This time, people stopped to listen and gladly received the tracts. It was obvious that a spiritual stronghold had been broken. A post script to that story came to me some years later when I learned that William the Conqueror is one of my ancestors on my mother's side. I suppose that gave me a little extra authority for breakthrough in that incident.

Once we had completed our redeeming assignments, we joined Sister Gwen at the Paris Convention. She called us up to testify about our trip, and we shared about the amazing time we had had redeeming the D-Day landings beaches and how God had met us. When we had finished our story, an elderly lady stood up and waved her hand asking if she could come to the platform and share. Sister Gwen invited her up, and she proceeded to share that she, as a young woman, was one of Rees Howells' intercessors who interceded with him during the war, and that post war he had sent her and another intercessor to Normandy to intercede. He told them specifically to pray over the D-Day landing beaches, "because one day God is going to send a group of people that will set those beaches free." The lady ended by saying, "Today I have heard the fulfillment of the prophetic word by Rees Howells!"

When we returned home, we learned that when we were redeeming at the beaches of Normandy, ETH Debbie Galey received a song from the Lord:

> Normandy! The Spirit cries out, Normandy!
> Your beaches have bled for years
> They've cried many tears.
> But now you're free, Normandy!
> Now you're free, Normandy!
> Now you're free!

We returned to France on our way to Israel and had a wonderful Convention in Paris. On the return trip through Paris, we learned that a hurricane had driven through the English Channel—highly unusual!

Sometime later we learned from Colin Wilkinson that the hurricane had destroyed the meeting places of the witches covens that had been meeting regularly in that area. He also told us of some British Lydia Prayer ladies that went annually to the England side of the English Channel to pray. They had always seen a terrible spiritual darkness as they looked across the Channel toward France. When they came the year that we had redeemed the land on the Normandy beaches, they saw angels instead. Glory to God!

The Delivery

On my first visit to the obstetrician, he declared upon examining me that I was a good candidate for a C-Section. I told him that although I may be small boned, my husband also was, so I was sure that I would be able to have this baby normally. Due to this threat, however, we decided not to try to have the baby at home with a midwife, since the nearest hospital is about 45-50 minutes drive from home.

Philip and I dutifully attended Lamaze classes and practiced coaching and breathing and relaxing. My beloved sister, Carole, had volunteered to come when we got close to the delivery time. When she arrived, we did some things together in preparation. I also had to finish typesetting something that Sister Gwen gave me orders to finish before the baby came ☺.

About 4:30 a.m., I awoke with a great deal of discomfort and realized that I was having contractions. A couple of hours later I had another sign that it was labor, and we called the doctor around 7:00 a.m. to notify him that the contractions were coming about three to five minutes apart, although they were not extremely regular. He told us to come to the hospital. I dilly-dallied as long as possible because I didn't want to have to stop eating. I knew that once I got there, I would only be given ice chips until the baby was born, and I didn't want to face having to do all that labor without any sustenance. I had had some trouble with hypoglycemia and wanted to be careful not to have a sugar low. Since the doctor was so convinced that I was a good candidate for a C-Section, I knew that food would be off limits.

I had a good breakfast, and Mary Ellen made me some carrot juice to take along. We sat in the hospital parking lot, and I drank carrot juice until I couldn't wait any longer. When I checked in, the nurse told me I was dilated about two to four centimeters. When I got settled in a bed on a monitor, the contractions slowed down to almost nothing. I got up and walked around for a while, but without much action.

After a while, the nurse informed me that the doctor would be over during his lunch hour to break my water. I replied, "I don't want him to break my water!"

"You don't? Why not?"

"Because I know that if he breaks my water and that doesn't work, that he'll give me pitocin [drug used to induce labor], and if that doesn't work, he'll do a C-Section, and I don't want a C-Section!"

"Well, I guess you know the ropes!" she said, and called the doctor back.

When he showed up on his lunch hour, he was not a happy camper! "I thought you wanted to have this baby today," he said angrily.

"I'm not in a hurry," I said. "Let it come when it's ready."

After checking my progress, he said, "You might as well go home."

I replied, "That's great! I'd rather labor at home anyway."

"You're not in labor."

"I'm not?"

"No, the definition of labor is contractions that bring forth dilation that brings forth birth, and you are not dilating."

So with a mixture of relief and disappointment, I got dressed, and we got in the van to go home. About the time we reached Dogpatch (fifteen minutes from Harrison where the hospital is located), the contractions started again, but only occasionally.

By this time I was hungry and exhausted. Mary Ellen made me lunch and while I was eating my tomato soup and grilled cheese sandwich, Sister Gwen called. When she found out that I had come home from the hospital, she was incensed and concerned.

She gave orders for us to go back to Harrison and check into a motel to wait it out until the baby came. I was so sleepy that I begged to be allowed to take a nap. I woke up to major contractions! By this time, Philip had started printing the book cover for *Paradise, the Holy City and the Glory of the Throne,*[12] so I just settled into Grandma Cain's platform rocker and Carole coached me. "Make your hands relax. Make your jaw relax. Take a deep breath…count…now let it out slowly…count…" This went on all afternoon and into the evening while Philip printed.

About 11:00 p.m. he came in and I said, "Let's just go to the hospital and let them check my progress. If I'm not far enough along, we'll go check into a motel." We got loaded in the van and Philip had to stop three times going up the hill while I had contractions.

Now they had told us in Lamaze class that the time will come during labor that "it will feel good to push." By the time we were going past Dogpatch, I could feel that my body was starting to push involuntarily. I said, "I—can't—keep—from—pushing!" Philip stepped on the gas and ran the red light as we came into town. I had a hard time getting out of the van because the contractions were coming so rapidly. When the nurse checked my progress in the Emergency Room around 12:15 a.m., she said, "Ten centimeters and bulging!"

They took me up to the Obstetrics Department and put me in a labor room. When the doctor showed up (none too happy for having been awakened), he broke my water (I was ready for it by then), told me to start pushing and then left. Now it was

12 See EngeltalPress.com or call (870) 446-2665 to order.

91

Philip's turn to coach me. The lab technician showed up to take a blood sample, and I made him stop until I finished having a contraction—wondering why this couldn't have been done when I had been there hours earlier.

After about 45 minutes, they rolled me into the delivery room and our daughter was born. I was miffed that my glasses had been left in the car. When the doctor said, "It's a girl!" I was stunned as I thought I was going to have a boy. I was even more stunned at how beautiful she was, and my first words were, "She's beautiful!" I had no idea a newborn could be that beautiful—but she was. And I'm sure that it's not just that she was my baby! She cried with tremendous strength—then all of a sudden she opened her eyes and began to look around. She stopped crying immediately as she began to take in her new world. They weighed her in at seven pounds and measured 21 inches in length. After she took her vitals, the nurse gave her to me. I was such a happy mommy! She was born December 4, 1987 at 1:07 a.m.

A few weeks earlier, Carolyn Wright, who did the portrait of Sister Gwen on her autobiography, *Unconditional Surrender,* asked me what we were going to call the baby. I replied, "Ian," certain that I would have a boy.

She said with a great deal of authority, "You'd better get a girl's name!"

It had been a toss-up between Aimee (for Aimee Semple McPherson) and Heather (knowing that Sister Gwen had wanted to have a girl named Heather, but had only had boys). So Philip and I had agreed together that we would use the name Heather. Now we were faced with the question of what to use for a middle name. Should we use Elaine after my mother or Elizabeth, which is my middle name. After saying the names over and over, we liked the sound of Heather Elizabeth Buss.

When we brought her home, Linda Hartzell took one look at her and said, "She looks so old—like she has a great depth of wisdom in her!"

Just like her mommy, she became a traveler at a young age. We started out on a lengthy series of regional conventions when she was ten weeks old. By the time we returned home in May, she had been in 27 states and two provinces of Canada.

God brought End-Time Handmaiden, Betty Hill, to us sovereignly to be Heather's nanny. She had many years of experience as a Bible smuggler behind the Iron Curtain and in China. She travelled with us and lived upstairs in our home for Heather's first year. She was wonderful with Heather. After she left us, she went on to be a missionary in Mongolia shortly after the nation opened when Communism fell in the Soviet Union.

Heather was a great traveler on her first and second trips to Israel: the first in utero (they almost didn't let me on the plane to go home!) and the second when she was nine months old.

Accounting

When Heather was still a baby, we had a shift in the staff, and I ended up having to be in charge of the accounting department. I was already wearing plenty of hats, so what was one more? I was quite intimidated by the prospect, though, as I didn't like math. Then it was explained to me that accounting is really just accounting for where the money goes. Well, that was different! Then it was no longer a matter of math, but a matter of integrity, and that I could handle!

Heather's First Sentence

When Heather was about seven months old, Betty Hill was rolling her along in her stroller one afternoon when we were at a Christian Booksellers Convention. They encountered another child in a stroller and Heather said, "Hi, baby!"

She wasn't always a smiling baby, although it wasn't too hard to get one out of her. It seemed that she was frustrated that she couldn't express herself.

When it came time for the annual spring trip when she was seventeen months old, I stayed home with Heather and Philip drove alone with the books. Early one morning, she surprised me with a conversation beyond what she had ever spoken before. I heard her wake up, and I quietly listened and watched from beyond the end of her bed where we couldn't actually see each other, but I could see into the room. All at once, her pacifier flew across the room. We always called it a "pluggie," but she called it a "baba." I said, "Heather, what happened to your pluggie?"

She replied, "I thew it doyn. I thew it, the baba." Wow! Up to that point she had only said one or two words together!

The more she learned to talk, the happier she got. We allowed her to answer the intercom at home. She would say, "Buss rebisence." I thought that was so cute!

Jasper United Methodist Church

That summer, Philip and I were invited to sing at the Jasper United Methodist Church while their choir was on vacation. We gave it our best to sing the Gospel and uphold the Blood of Jesus in our songs. We were delighted to find that the new pastor, Rev. Larry Hunt, was a fiery preacher who had come to the United Methodist denomination via the General Baptist, with his deep roots as a boy preacher in the Church of the Nazarene. We felt that the Lord wanted us to get behind this man of God

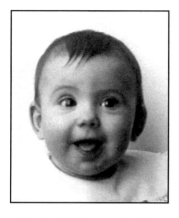

Heather's first passport photo; she looks like the "Gerber Baby"!

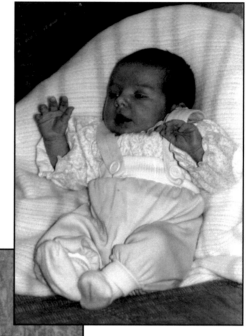

Heather Elizabeth Buss, three days old

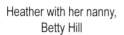

Heather with her nanny, Betty Hill

At ten weeks old, she's ready for her first road trip. By the time she was five months old, she had been in 27 states and two provinces of Canada.

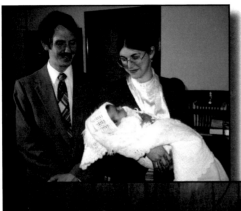

We dedicated Heather to the Lord before she was born, but we also presented her to Him once again at our first International School of Ministry (ISOM).

Grandpa and Grandma Buss enjoy a moment with two out of four granddaughters, Serena and Heather.

Grandma and Grandpa Parks meet their fifth great-granddaughter

and start attending there. I remember Heather putting two nickels in the "birthday bank" on her second birthday.

Pastor Hunt soon had the place filled up every Sunday morning, with the narthex opened up and chairs added up the center aisle. He approached us to announce his intentions of starting an early service and asked if we would consider leading the singing for it. He wanted it to be a bit more "evangelical" and the 11:00 a.m. service would continue to be more liturgical. We agreed to do so, and both services continued to grow.

Occasionally we had to leave Heather at home for a week or two or three, but as she got older, we were able to bring her with us more.

Plenty of Things…

At one of the regional conventions in Washington, DC, our ETH Joyce Scott, missionary to India, announced that she and Bill were retiring. I was incensed! I had to slip out of the meeting about that time and began fussing at the Lord. "They can't just leave that work! It's so vital to be printing the Gospel for the masses! I know all about printing. I was born in India. I have a burden for India. I'm capable of doing that job—" I was volunteering to the Lord.

His thundering voice spoke within my spirit, "There are plenty of things you are capable of doing that I've not called you to do!"

Well that let the air out of my puffed up balloon in a hurry! I got the message, and have tried to be careful ever since, as I have always had a tendency to take on things that I know I can do just because it seems they should, or at least could, be done. Not long after that I found a motto that I hung in my office. It said, "There is no point doing well that which you should not be doing at all!"

Heather always had a bit of a prophetic bent. There were two occasions when she begged to stay the night at Grandma and Grandpa Buss' house. Each time it was critical that Philip and I were unencumbered so that we could handle emergency situations. One of them was when we had to take a sister with internal bleeding to the hospital in the middle of the night. On the way there, we realized that she was rapidly slipping from earth to Heaven and we called her back. Thankfully, she recovered and is still serving the Lord in Argentina.

The Fire

The other time that it happened was the night of November 16/17, 1990. We were nearing the end of a session of our International School of Ministry (ISOM). I was in charge of the accounting department at the time, but was also busy with the meetings. So when Heather cried and begged to go home with Grandma and Grandpa, I was a bit relieved as I had work to do in the office and was happy for the opportunity to get some things done. A little after midnight, I finished up in the office, and stopped in to visit Sister Gwen for a few minutes before going home. A man that had come to the school had been rushed to the hospital that evening, and we had just gotten a call from the hospital with the update when suddenly the phone call was cut off. We checked all the lines and they were dead. We were mystified at the cause, then we heard the screams and shouts of "Fire! Fire! Qumran's on fire!"

We ran to see and found our office building was burning at the south end where the phone system control panel was. So that's why the phone had been cut off! We had no way of calling for help! Papa Jim and I realized that the flames hadn't reached the main part of the office yet, so we tried desperately to enter the building to get out whatever we could save. When we entered from the lower level, we were stopped by the smoke and darkness. The electricity was already out as the power lines also came into the building at the south end.

Then we went around to the upper level and tried to enter again, but again, we were stopped by the smoke, even though we tried to crawl in. I remembered that the computer backups were right by the window, so Steve Leigh ran for a ladder and climbed up to break the glass and retrieve them. Marylois Little and Sandy Kalland broke windows in the new bookstore area and managed to retrieve a few mottos before the smoke made them give up as well.

Then I ran back to Sister Gwen's house where the decision was made to evacuate the valley. It was autumn and all the leaves were dead and dry. We hadn't had any rain for some time. The place was a tinder box! We were concerned about the propane tank behind the building, and felt we should get everyone out while we could still get them past the burning building. We loaded up one of the vans with people and Sister Gwen said, "Let's go to Dorothy's."

So vehicle after vehicle went up the hill, not knowing what would be left when we got back. I was mostly concerned with getting Sister Gwen to a safe place with the few belongings that she had hurriedly gathered. I hadn't taken the time to go home at all, so I briefly pondered that I might only have the clothes on my back by morning—but I was so relieved to know that Heather was safe at Grandma and Grandpa's! I marveled at how the Lord had put that desire in her heart! He is so faithful!

We pulled up to Dorothy and Estel's house and banged on the door. By this time it was after one a.m. They came and let us in as the tragic story tumbled out of our mouths. The commotion also woke up Heather and she was so happy to see me, and I was so happy that she had begged to come to Grandma's!

When we got settled, Sister Gwen said, "Dorothy, go to the piano and play something for us." She sat down and played, "Bless the Lord, O my soul and all that is within me, bless His holy name." We sang together with shattered hearts, knowing that God was still sovereign. Like Job said, "Though He slay me, yet will I trust Him!"

About that time, Pastor Hunt showed up. He had heard the news from one of his parishioners that lived on the mountain above us and immediately came to be with us and comfort us. There is nothing like the "ministry of presence" in a time of tragedy—it's not the words you say so much as just being there that brings comfort to the soul. After singing with us for a while, he went down to the valley and spent the rest of the night with Philip and Papa Jim and those brave souls who had opted to stay and keep the fire from spreading.

Thankfully, the angels were busy that night. Somehow the Deer, Arkansas volunteer Fire Department had gotten word and they came out to help. The propane tank never did explode and, although you could see flaming pieces of paper flying through the air, the woods surrounding Qumran never caught fire. When it was all over, burned pages of Sister Gwen's books were found two miles away.

Everything in the building was consumed: the computers (our first three—it was rather new technology) typesetter (that had been a very expensive investment!), electric typewriters and word processors, the video camera and brand new editing suite, the bookstore and tape duplicating department, the library full of books, the 70,000 sheets of brand new paper (one third of a semi truck load) that we had just purchased for printing books, all the printing equipment—everything! Philip recalls hearing the huge camera we used for making the lithographic negatives for printing when the floor gave way under it and it crashed to the lower level. A couple of weeks after the fire, Philip discovered a white patch in his hair that hadn't been there before. One sister said that was where God touched him on the head the night of the fire.

Sister Gwen had just completed putting a huge amount of her photos into albums just days earlier and they all burned. Helen Hilley, Marylois Little's mother, volunteered to do all my months worth of filing for me during the school and had just finished hours before the fire. I guess God wanted it all in order before it went to Heaven!

The next day we sent the students home after a time of sharing and prayer. Everyone was devastated, but Sister Gwen took it the hardest. She was within about a month of her fifty-year anniversary in the ministry. She had planned to take a sabbatical, but this forced her to start a month early. The first thing that the Lord spoke to Sister Gwen after the fire was, "Full stop!"

A day or two later, Philip, Heather and I stopped in to see Sister Gwen. She was sitting in the corner chair in her living room looking dazed and dejected. Heather walked up to her in her nearly three-year-old way, put her hand on Sister Gwen's and began to sing, "Onward Christian Soldiers." It was truly a message from Heaven to encourage her not to give up hope. "Out of the mouths of babes...hath God perfected praise."

Another message of encouragement in that time of tragedy came from Marylois. She brought one of the mottos she had pulled from the bookstore to Sister Gwen. It had a photo of a natural rock bridge and barren, rocky cliffs by a river. Written below the photo was, "Do not remember the former things, nor consider the things of old. Behold, I will do a new thing, now it shall spring forth; Shall you not know it? I will even make a road in the wilderness and rivers in the desert. Isaiah 43:18, 19"

Marylois felt that she should stay with Sister Gwen for some days after all the students left. Papa Jim had previously made arrangements to drive to New York with Frank Sellinger to purchase a van from ETH Pearl McLain, and didn't feel that he should postpone it. Marylois was a great blessing to Sister Gwen while he was gone. She soon made arrangements for the rest of the family to move to Jasper, so they could be with us to help.

Except for Papa Jim's, Qumran had contained all our offices. It also housed the print shop, the warehouse, the bookstore, the tape duplication department, the video editing suite, the ISOM offices, the desktop publishing, etc. Since all of that was gone, we no longer needed all the staff for all those departments, so Sister Gwen had to let them go.

Philip and I personally lost some treasures in the fire. Both our guitars had been left in the classroom as we were expecting to lead praise and worship in the morning. We had also left our study Bibles and notebooks in the classroom and I had another favorite Bible in my office. Many of my favorite photographs that I had taken were on my wall in my office. My dad had only recently given me my baby pictures, and I had them in the office to show to my co-workers. To this day we occasionally think of an item that we lost in the fire. A bit of my desire for photography was lost when I lost those photos. I still take pictures, but not with the zeal I once had.

Funeral for Qumran

Shortly after the fire, Cliff Dudley called Sister Gwen and told her that he felt the Lord wanted him to come to Engeltal and conduct a "funeral" for Qumran. So we gathered together with a few friends and prayed and sang and eulogized. Cliff was a great blessing and with that service, much of the mourning lifted off of us.

After Sister Gwen completed her year of sabbatical rest and writing, her ministry travels mostly took her overseas, and she travelled with only Papa Jim to help her. We couldn't take the van there to carry books, after all. She rarely travelled in the United States, except for her annual visit to Blue Mountain Christian Retreat in Pennsylvania. So we settled down in Engeltal and kept busy there. Although it was painful not to get to go with Sister Gwen so much, in retrospect, I can see the hand of God keeping us at home to give Heather greater stability as she was growing up.

Publishing after the Fire

Soon after the fire, Ernest Mall came to visit and comfort Sister Gwen in her loss. He had been her tent manager in India in the 1960's and had since moved to Chicago and developed a printing business. I believe that he and Karl had learned printing in the same place. By this time, his business was thriving and he had begun printing books as well. He promised that he would help us get all the books printed again. He was such a wonderful comfort in that time and allowed us to pay the bills over a period of time since there were so many projects to do all at once. We have always been grateful to him for stepping in to help like that.

Not long after the fire, the Lord spoke to Sister Gwen, "Build a print shop." It seemed apparent that He didn't mean to rebuild Qumran yet. The pile of ashes still sat there mocking us. No, this was to be something smaller, just to house the printing. We had taken a step of faith to just get some tracts printed commercially in the area and were shocked to see the price!

Papa Jim began looking around for a building rather than starting from scratch to build one here in Engeltal. He found an empty metal building up on the top of the hill, and we purchased it. It was perfect for what we needed to do. Philip and I quickly set out shopping for equipment and Ernest helped us look. Before long it was fully furnished and functional, only now Philip was in charge of the whole thing as I had my hands full with the accounting department.

In one night the building was destroyed that housed our offices, bookstore, warehouse, print shop, School of Ministry, audio and video production, library and so much more.

Cliff Dudley officiated at the "funeral" for Qumran.

This family portrait was taken a short time after the fire. Heather was three.

ETH&S Joyce and Larry Groves had attended the ISOM leading up to the fire. She felt to stay on to be the "nanny" for Heather, Josiah Schmidt, and Gavin Doorn. Larry went home to go back to work at RR Donnelley, a well-known printing company, where he was a supervisor. The Lord began to deal with him to retire early, sell their house, and come to Engeltal. When they came on staff full time, Larry became a pressman in the printshop and soon learned all the steps necessary to produce the "Angel Letters," tracts and magazines. I want to see the multitudes in Heaven who got there because of Larry's obedience to God. He has printed thousands upon thousands upon thousands of "Who Is Jesus?" tracts.

Temporary Offices

At the time of the fire, Sister Gwen was having a room built on to her house. It was nearly finished, so instead of becoming what she had planned, it was turned into an office. One of the bedrooms in her house was turned into the accounting office.

The day after the fire, our nearest neighbors came to Sister Gwen's door with a box of pencils, pens, paper, and other items as a gift. They realized we had absolutely nothing with which to conduct business and were moved by compassion to help us. How kind of them!

Papa Jim and I went to the newly opened Office Depot in Springfield, Missouri, to outfit us with more of the things we would need. It was a novelty to us at that time to have such a store with virtually everything we could need under one roof.

I went shopping for two computers—our first laptops to be able to start back to work. Before long we bought two more desktop computers as well. We were able to get the program and data restored from the disks that we had rescued from the window of the accounting office as the building was burning, thank God!

Kayla

One of the children that attended Sunday School with Heather was a little girl named Kayla. One of her parents would drop her off for the lesson and came back later to get her.

Winter in the Ozarks is much milder than further north, but we are often on the line between snow to the north and rain to the south. That means ice or a wintery mix for us. Our mountainous terrain makes the roads curvy and sometimes steep. One icy, snowy afternoon, I was working in the temporary office at Sister Gwen's as the freezing rain and snow mix was falling all around. I suddenly heard what sounded like thunder, and I thought it was odd. After some time passed, I volunteered to take Betty Coates to her home on the other side of the mountain. We had a four-wheel drive vehicle and I knew how to drive in wintery conditions, so I wasn't concerned.

As we approached the Cliff House, I could see that there had been an accident. A propane truck had hit a car head on. All the officials were seeing to the situation, so I just took Betty home and returned to Engeltal.

Later we learned that Pastor Hunt had been the only customer in a little café in town that late afternoon. It was run by Kayla's daddy and Kayla was there with him. Pastor Hunt was talking to him seriously about making things right with God, but he was not yet ready to make a commitment.

After Pastor Hunt left, the man closed the place and left with his four-year-old daughter and headed up the mountain to go home. If I recall correctly, the propane truck lost control on the slippery road and caused the collision. Kayla was killed instantly, and her daddy died about an hour or two later.

The whole community was grieving this loss of two precious souls. I was so deeply burdened for the family and prayed for them with weeping. When I finished, the Holy Spirit gave me a beautiful ballad. The first and last verses are from the familiar "Jesus Loves Me."

Song for Kayla

Jesus loves me this I know
For the Bible tells me so.
Little ones to Him belong.
They are weak but He is strong.

There's a new little girl in Paradise today,
Her name is Kayla.
The angels quickly brought her
And for eternity she'll stay,
Precious little Kayla.

For only as a child can we enter in.
The gates of Heaven are reserved
For those set free from sin.
Jesus' blood can wash away everything that's wrong
And make us just like little ones
That to Him belong.

"Jesus, will my daddy be coming soon to me?"
Asked little Kayla.
"We're giving him a chance to pray,
"We're waiting now to see,
"My precious Kayla.

"For only as a child can he enter in.
"The gates of Heaven are reserved
"For those set free from sin.
"O My blood can wash away everything that's wrong
"And make him too My little one
"That to Me belongs."

"Well, what about my mommy
And all those by her side?"
Asked little Kayla.

"I have sent My angels, and I surely will provide,
"My precious Kayla."

"For only as a child can they enter in.
The gates of Heaven are reserved
For those set free from sin.
"I'll restore their innocence
And wash away what's wrong
"And make them too My little ones
"That to Him belong."

And so to bring us to this place of decision here today,
Jesus needed Kayla.
She makes us look to Heaven,
And she makes us want to pray,
Don't disappoint sweet Kayla!

For only as a child can we enter in.
The gates of Heaven are reserved
For those set free from sin.
Jesus' blood can wash away everything that's wrong
And make us just like little ones
That to Him belong.

Jesus loves me He will stay,
Close beside me all the way.
If I love Him, when I die,
He will take me home on high.

I was able to sing it to the family after the funeral. I pray that the Lord used it to touch their hearts.

Later we recorded it as a family. Heather, who was four at the time, sang the Kayla parts, Philip sang the Jesus parts, and I sang the narrator parts. Tommy Schmidt included it on a CD he compiled called, "A Strange Way to Save the World."

Heather Sees a Vision

Due to Pastor Hunt's loving pastoral care the night of the fire, Sister Gwen and Papa Jim became members of the Jasper United Methodist Church and attended regularly when they were home. Sunday School was held in between the services and normally we attended, but Sister Gwen and Papa Jim didn't. On one occasion, Heather didn't want to go to Sunday School—that was not normal! So Sister Gwen said, "Don't worry, we'll take her home with us so that you can go. Just stop by the house and pick her up when you get back."

When we returned, Sister Gwen told us that while Heather was passing the time, she looked over at the yellow house we call "Edelweiss" where Sister Gwen's mother lived. "Mom Bergman," as everyone called her was in her 90's and had become quite frail. Heather said, "Nanny, I see Mom Bergman with a sheet over her head." That was Sister Gwen's first clue that the Lord would shortly be taking her mother Home to be with Him. Not long after that, she began talking about these people who told her that "it would be easier for her if she didn't eat." So she left off eating most of the time. The last meal that she had with us was Thanksgiving dinner, and then she suffered a stroke. In a matter of days, she peacefully breathed her last while we all stood around and sang hymns of Heaven to her. Heather told me years later that she knew what the sheet over the head meant, but she didn't want to say it to Nanny.

Travelling with Heather

While I had been sitting in the accounting office, my heart had begun to burn for Scotland. I wept and travailed for the Lord to send us there. Charlen and Glenn Logemann made arrangements for us to go to Scotland the summer after the fire, Philip, Heather, and I flew into London and went up to Sedley Pimlott's church in Norwich for a convention. Then we rented a car and drove to Peterhead to be with our ETH Jane Strachen. Jane toured us around the country, having arranged meetings in various places where we ministered. We ate fish and chips nearly every day and loved it. We also prayed and redeemed the land with her in some important places.

It was August and most folks were on vacation. You had to arrive early in a place to be able to get a room for the night in a bed and breakfast. One night we were planning to stay in Inverness, but didn't get there early enough. We drove all over trying to find a place to stay. Nothing was available there or anywhere along Loch Ness and beyond. Finally, we drove toward the ferry that would take us to our next destination, the Isle of Skye, which is situated off the west coast of Scotland. We parked there for the remainder of the night and slept in the car until the first ferry in the morning. It rained all night, and the car was small, so it wasn't very restful. When daylight came, we saw nearby a tent with bicycles beside it. We wondered which group of us had slept better—the ones who could stretch out or the ones who were dry!

When we arrived at our host's home in the early morning, they welcomed us and let us take a nap before breakfast. Angus, our host, apologized that he only had some salmon to serve us that he had just caught in the Atlantic from his back yard. We were so thrilled with it that we couldn't imagine him apologizing, but for him it was just the ordinary fare.

It rains a lot on Skye. We were told that if you are standing on the mainland and you can see Skye, it's going to rain. If you can't see Skye, it's already raining. Because of all the rain, we saw lots of rainbows.

Heather was a real trooper on that trip and took it all well. She was a good traveler.

Bill Grogan's Goat

When I was a child I learned the song "Bill Grogan's Goat."

TAKE THE LID OFF

Josiah turned four in November, Heather turned three in December, and Gavin turned four in January. We had one cake tor all three.

One day Heather said to me, "Mommy, I'm three and four."

I said, "No, you are three. How could you be three and four?"

"That's the way God made me," she replied.

Sister Gwen with the youngsters of the Little, Schmidt, and Buss households.

Bryan, Alysa, Joy
Josiah, Heather, Sister Gwen, Cola, and Jason.

Heather with a real Highland bagpiper

Heather in the heather in Scotland

111

BILL GROGAN'S GOAT

Bill Grogan's goat
Was feeling fine
Ate three red shirts
Right off the line

Bill took a stick
Gave him a whack,
And tied him to
The railroad track.

The whistle blew
The train was nigh
Bill Grogan's goat
Was doomed to die!

He gave a cough
Of mortal pain,
Coughed up those shirts
And flagged the train!

Author Unknown

During an event we were holding in the chapel in Engeltal, Philip and I were leading the worship, and Sister Gwen was playing the organ. I had prayerfully prepared the song list, and just knew that this was what the Holy Spirit wanted us to do. It had such a good flow from one song to the next. Everything was going well, the Holy Spirit was moving, and people were being blessed in the worship.

Suddenly, Sister Gwen took over and began leading in a different direction with different songs. I began to boil inside because this was contrary to what I thought the Lord had in mind, when in actuality, I was angry and frustrated because I had lost control. The Lord in His lovingkindness and tender mercies whispered sweetly in my spirit, "You can sing 'Bill Grogan's Goat,' and if I anoint it, it's anointed."

Well, I had to smile and chuckle at the very notion, but I knew the Voice, and His words diffused my so-called "righteous indignation." It was important for me to stay in the anointing so the worship wouldn't be disrupted in the spirit realm.

Not long after that, during an ISOM, Ruthie, a sweet lady from Kentucky stood up and said that she kept hearing a song in the spirit, so Sister Gwen encouraged her to sing it. We were all floored when she began singing, "She'll Be Comin' Around the Mountain When She Comes." She then explained that it was all about the Bride and the Bridegroom. My previous experience with the Lord's humor opened my heart to this new prophetic viewpoint of an old children's song.

Eternal Goals — "Well, Honey..."

When I was in my thirties, I began a practice of writing what I called, "Taking Stock," around the time of my birthday each year. I would put down what I felt were my accomplishments of my life up to that point and pondered my goals. Eventually, it became discouraging, because I couldn't see that I was getting anywhere with my "goals" in life.

In my earlier years at Engeltal, I had read two books that impacted me deeply: *Aimee* by Aimee Semple McPherson, and *Diary of Signs and Wonders* by Maria Woodworth Etter. As I read of their mighty campaigns where multitudes were saved, filled with the Holy Spirit, healed and changed by the power of God, my heart was profoundly stirred. I could see myself doing that kind of thing. Whenever Sister Gwen would preach about revival, I always felt an intense fire awakening in my spirit. I wanted to be a revivalist.

So on one of these occasions when I was "taking stock," I became disheartened about it. About that time, June Lewis, one of our wonderful teachers from our International School of

Ministry called. I took advantage of the opportunity to bend her ear with my complaints about not reaching my goals in life.

She drawled, "Well, Honey, your problem is that you are setting goals for the here and now. What are your eternal goals? That's what you should be working on!"

I thought, "Eternal goals? I didn't even know you could have eternal goals!" So in the ensuing days, I pondered what my eternal goals ought to be. The conclusion I reached was that if I could truly set eternal goals, I wanted to be on the worship team at the throne of God for eternity. So, I no longer had to wonder about what I might have to do to get on a platform and preach to thousands with signs, wonders, and miracles for a season of my earthly life. Now all that was important to me was to live my life in such a way that I would line up with the Word of God and cultivate my relationship with Him to the degree that would qualify me to dwell at the throne for eternity. That changed everything for me! I began to realize that it's not so much that we want God to acknowledge what we have done for Him in this life, but that it was done well. We want to hear Him say, "Well done, thou good and faithful servant...enter into the joy of thy Lord" (Matthew 25:21, 23). Not just, "Well, you did this and you did that, but..."

I would not be surprised to eventually find myself ministering to great crowds and seeing the signs, wonders, and miracles that I was imagining. I believe God put that vision inside me. But if you don't have the intimate relationship with God and have His character built inside you, having a great anointing and doing the supernatural won't get you to the throne for eternity. In Matthew 7:22-23, Jesus declared that He would say to some who had performed miracles in His Name, "I never knew you: depart from me, ye that work iniquity."

As the Apostle Paul expressed in Philippians 3:10, I want to "know Him and the power of His resurrection, and the fellowship of His sufferings, being made conformable unto His death." I want Him to have full rule and reign in every area of my life so that He can take over and do whatever He wants to do.

China

In November of 1991, Brother Wallace Helfin invited Sister Gwen and Papa Jim to come on his tour of China. Several other End-Time Handmaidens were also planning on going. Once again I sat in my accounting office aching to go to China with Sister Gwen. I felt that I had an appointment with God there, and I couldn't shake it. At the very last possible day, I went to Sister Gwen and told her the burden of my heart. God miraculously supplied the finances and by a miracle the travel agent was able to get me a ticket. The tour was leaving on Monday, and I had opened my heart about it on Friday—it was an amazing "suddenly."

Normally when we were on tour, I was the tour coordinator and photographer. This time I had no responsibilities and through a communications breakdown, I didn't have my camera. My joining the group had made an odd number of ladies, so at first I had a room all to myself. This WAS an appointment with God!

We toured all over the land and prayed as we went. I so look forward to getting to Heaven to see the "video replays" of all the unseen spiritual warfare! One morning as I was sitting all alone in my room just quietly enjoying the Lord, I was telling Him, "I love you, Lord," when I heard that Voice again in my spirit saying, "I love you, too." What a deeply moving moment! I realized that I had been so busy with all the work that I was doing for God that it had been a long time since I had heard His voice like that. But He loved me enough to cause my heart to burn to go to the other side of the world and be stripped of all my responsibilities and hobbies to get me still enough to hear Him tell me of His love. Wow!

That is not to say that I hadn't been hearing from Him at all. He often guides me by hearing a song or a scripture in my spirit, But I was so grateful to hear His Voice like that and that He had gone to such extremes to give me a break so He could minister to me in that way.

It was also on this tour that I had my first opportunity to smuggle the Word of God to the hungry saints in China. We had distributed thousands of "Who Is Jesus?" tracts throughout the tour group. One night after dinner, I went from door to door, collecting them in my backpack. Then I went to Sister Gwen's room and unloaded to go back for more. Now in China, the hotels have a "service desk" on each floor so the personnel can keep an eye on what's going on. I don't know what they were thinking while I was going from room to room, but I was thinking, "I was born for this!" I felt such a wonderful excitement and fulfilling of my dream to smuggle Bibles.

When the load was all collected, Papa Jim put them in a suitcase and we headed out the door with a man who was living in the area to take them to their first destination. When we entered the home of the network contact, we saw piles of literature against the wall. Thankfully, she was a well educated woman, actually a doctor by training before the Revolution, and she could speak excellent English. A young woman from the network had arrived to pick up a load and head back immediately to the train station to take her precious cargo to a distant city for distribution. This girl had laid aside everything to be doing this kind of work, and it had great risk to her life and freedom. We marveled at the price that these saints were willing to pay for the Gospel, for love of the Master. It was deeply moving for me and profoundly impacted my life.

I carefully journaled through the whole trip, keeping record of all the details. I have been grateful to be able to go back and read my notes of that time. One significant point was that I felt the Lord was telling me that one day I would be leading tours to the nations as Brother Heflin did and that our ministries would become more closely related. It wasn't long after that tour that Sister Gwen became an annual speaker at Calvary Pentecostal Tabernacle Camp in Ashland, Virginia, headed by Brother Heflin.

Cuba

During this season, other than the annual trip to Israel, we rarely made overseas trips with Sister Gwen. In 1993, Sister Gwen felt a burden from the Lord for Mexico and Cuba, and wanted us to come along. He led us to connect with Ruth Coffey in Cuernavaca, Mexico, through ETH Shirley Smith. We had glorious meetings there and the Holy Spirit really impacted lives.

We then flew on to Cuba with ETS Lester Pedraza from Monterrey, Mexico, with us as the interpreter. He was a tour guide in Monterrey, as well as an evangelist, so he put on all his identification pins that showed he was a guide, and when we landed at the airport, he declared to the customs officials, "I am a guide and these are my people. This is my first time in your country. If you treat me well, I will bring more tour groups." It worked—we were hastened through customs without one suitcase being opened, hallelujah!

We were carrying tracts and Sister Gwen's Bible studies in Spanish, as well as soaps, shampoos and toothbrushes for the saints. We had heard that these items weren't available to the average Cuban, and wanted to help in a material way as well as spiritual.

Because communications were largely blocked to Cuba, it was difficult to get a message to them that our flight had been changed. In order to get a call through, I had to phone around 3:00 a.m. I managed to reach someone and passed on the message, however, that person didn't pass it on to the pastor. Consequently, there was no one to meet us at the airport. So we took two taxis with all our stuff. Sister Gwen, Papa Jim, and Brother Lester were in the first taxi and Philip and I were in the second. It was May Day and the Communists were having a parade. We managed to catch the very last of it.

The driver for the first taxi began telling his riders about himself. His father was Jewish, so Sister Gwen encouraged him to take us to the local synagogue. We were welcomed by the secretary and custodian as they were the only ones there. They showed us around and told us of their small Jewish community. They said they weren't especially singled out for persecution here and that they were allowed to receive packages from Canada containing the foods and other items they would need to celebrate Passover, etc. We chatted and finally blessed them with a few songs in Hebrew that Philip and I knew. We felt we were fulfilling the scripture, "To the Jew first…" After touring around a bit, we went and got settled in our hotel.

The buildings in Havana appeared as though they hadn't been painted for many years. The revolution was in 1959. The main mode of transportation appeared to be "Flying Pigeon" bicycles from China—hundreds of them were on the streets, sometimes carrying whole families. There were quite a few cars from the 1950's and a few smaller Eastern European models.

Just before we left Little Rock on this journey, Shirley Smith had been able to catch us on the plane before it took off to give us a box with a wedding dress in it. She had been to Cuba earlier and learned that the daughter of one of the pastors was getting married, but had no wedding dress. She asked if we would deliver it for her. So when we arrived and had no one to meet us, we looked in the wedding dress box and found an address and phone number. Brother Lester made a call and took another taxi ride to meet the pastor. From that point, we were able to connect with our original contact and we began numerous meetings in various churches.

Philip and I were asked where we might want to go. They had arranged an interpreter for us so that we could double the effectiveness of the team by splitting up sometimes. I said that we would be willing to go where no one else goes, so they took me at my word and sent us miles away from Havana to a tiny church that hadn't had a visitor for a long time. We had a glorious time with them.

Another meeting was held at the church of the pastor we met first. It was quite a distance from Havana proper and transportation for the average person to get there was difficult. To conserve energy, the government would cause blackouts in the evening—just at the time that churches might be trying to have a meeting. So, there we were in the dark, with only a Chinese version of a Coleman lantern for light. Philip was scheduled to preach, but the interpreter hadn't shown up. So I quickly breathed a prayer for grace and began to preach in Spanish myself.

By this time it had been about fifteen years since I studied Spanish, and I hadn't used it very much. My vocabulary was (and still is) fairly limited. Every time I go to a Spanish-speaking nation, I'm rusty at first, then by the time I've been there about two weeks, I get to the point that I start thinking in the language instead of having to try and interpret my thoughts from English to Spanish—then I come home and quit using it.

So I preached my message with only the first row or two of people being lit and the rest were in the dark. When the service was over, the interpreter walked up and congratulated me on my sermon! He had taken a bicycle part of the way, then a bus, then caught a ride on the back of a truck to be able to get there, and so, arrived late! It was a good experience for me.

The brother in charge of the meetings took a great risk and boldly arranged an open air meeting for Sister Gwen. It was the first one that he knew of, and it was glorious! Philip and I sang, and she preached like a house on fire! Only eternity will reveal the hearts and lives that were touched and changed.

Romania

When Sister Gwen came home from Romania in the summer, she said, "Sharon, I see you and Philip in Romania." We acted on that word and made arrangements to go there to help ETH Becky Walsh. We flew into Munich, Germany, and she met us at the airport. We spent a couple of days gathering food, clothes, and printed materials to take with us, and then started on our journey. We drove through Austria and Hungary to get there.

As we entered Hungary, we could feel the darkness increase, but when we crossed into Romania, we felt it intensify even more. It was as though we entered a broken, demoralized nation. It was two years after the Communist dictator had been overthrown, but the ravages of that regime were still evident. It seemed we had stepped back in time about fifty years. Although there were Eastern European vehicles, horse-drawn carts and ox carts were also common. Many people simply walked to reach their destinations. Trains looked fifty years old as well. Most of the houses were quaint, "Old Country" style homes, some had never had plumbing yet. Everywhere we looked, we saw things that had long since been broken and no attempt had been made to repair them.

Becky told us of an incident she had experienced. She went to a department store to buy a lamp. Before she purchased it, she plugged it in to try it. "It doesn't work!" she said to the sales lady.

"So take it home and fix it," was the reply.

"But it's brand new! It should work!" Becky insisted.

The lady threw up her hands and said, "This is Romania!"

Becky took us all over the country, ministering in churches and schools. It was nearing Christmas, so we were able to share

120

the good news of the Christmas story and give out tangerines, hats, and Precious Moments Bible story books.

In the little "German" village of Bratei, we carefully picked our way through the muddy streets to the Pentecostal church from the home of the German lady that had fed us dinner. She had been commenting about the short-haired American women that had come to minister in their country and she was incensed. In this culture, women would generally wear a "babushka" (scarf) on their heads when attending church. So I dutifully put my scarf on babushka style.

We were delighted with the orchestra of mandolins that played that night. When we were introduced, we came up to share a song, Philip with his guitar and me with my omnichord. As I slid the strap over my head, I inadvertently knocked my scarf off. A gasp went through the crowd. I wasn't sure if they were gasping because my scarf had fallen off, or because they could then see that my long hair was displayed in a braid across the top of my head. I quickly replaced my scarf and we played. Then Philip preached, and there was a tremendous move of the Holy Spirit and a wonderful altar call. I have wondered if losing my scarf that night perhaps helped to break the ice a bit to open their hearts to receive from us as they could see that we were more like them than they thought Americans could be.

When we were in Bucharest, we went to the train station to give clothing to the homeless. We had to dump it and run, or we would have been mobbed! We found eighteen homeless children and took them out to eat pizza. Unfortunately, the proprietor wouldn't let them into his restaurant, so we had to get the pizza "to go," and we gave it to them on the street.

In Galati (pronounced Galatz), we ministered in a church and a prison. Becky purchased half a ton of oranges to give to the prisoners. I'm sure that some of them had never seen an orange before. We sang and preached to them and some opened their hearts to the Lord.

We arrived in Timisoara (pronounced Timishuara) around the second anniversary of the revolution. It had begun in this city with 25,000 people gathering in the square, declaring, "God exists!" and praying the Lord's Prayer.

At this point, though, the situation was tense, because the people had expected their living conditions to improve more rapidly than what had occurred. They didn't realize all that had to be undone before it could be redone, and no one knew of any other way of life. They had been one of the Soviet satellite nations since 1944, and their previous history had been one of political corruption and rule by violence.

We prayed as we walked there that God would bring His peace into that nation by transforming hearts by the knowledge of Him.

U.A.E.

Sister Gwen received an invitation to come to the United Arab Emirates, a small federation of seven emirates. Each one is ruled by its hereditary emir, or ruler. It is located on the Persian Gulf on the southeast of the Arabian Peninsula, neighbored by Saudi Arabia, and Oman. The brother who invited her had heard her preach in India many years earlier, and knew that his people needed her ministry. The U.A.E. is funded by vast supplies of oil and natural gas. Most of the workers there are expatriates, that is, foreign workers from Asia.

In order to go there, we had to get new passports that had no stamps of Israel in them as the U.A.E. doesn't recognize Israel, and wouldn't permit anyone who had been there to come to their nation. We intended to go there after our Israel Tour during the Feast of Tabernacles that year. The Israelis understand the problem and stamped our visa on a separate paper, so that there was no evidence of our travel to Israel. June Lewis joined our team, and had also obtained a new passport.

TAKE THE LID OFF

During the tour, we had an afternoon free. It was just before Shabbat, and we were limited on time, using the local busses for transportation. A small group of us decided to go to the Western Wall (Wailing Wall) and then up to the Temple Mount. As we walked around on the Temple Mount, Sister June was teaching us about where different parts of the Temple used to be. We decided to take a few minutes to pray, and one lady was particularly insistent that June should take authority over the Prince of Persia. She didn't want to and didn't feel good about it, but the lady nagged her so much that she gave in.

When we reached the bus stop, June reached into her very large shoulder bag and took out her wallet, extracted the bus fare and thought she dropped it back in her shoulder bag. When we sat down on the bus, she looked for her wallet to put her change away, and couldn't find it. She began to panic, for in that wallet were her travellers cheques, her credit cards, and her brand new passport! Upon arriving at the hotel, we called the police to make a report and Philip jumped on another bus to go back and look for it, without success.

Shabbat began and we couldn't do anything to rectify the situation. The next day we were able to replace her travelers cheques and cancel her credit cards, but it was Sunday and the U.S. Consulate was closed. The next day we were able to get her a new passport, but it was generated with Jerusalem as the place of issue.

When the tour group left, we took an El Al flight to Cairo, Egypt. We had some hours there and checked in for the next flight. All of our passports were collected and we sat and waited. Presently, June's name was called. She went to the desk and received the news: "You cannot go to the U.A.E. with a passport issued in Jerusalem! Impossible!"

June had planned to stop in Cairo to minister on her way back from the U.A.E., so she contacted ETH Sophie Rizkalla to help her. She left us at the airport and began days of ministering and making arrangements to obtain her third new passport (they had already become expensive by that time).

We headed for Dubai and were met by our Brother Jacob Matthews who took us to the apartment where we would stay. When we entered the building, our passports were taken from us before we could move into our place. That was scary!

The Emir of Dubai was a progressive man, and he had given a piece of land for the expatriate workers to build their churches. Several buildings were together in one compound and multiple congregations shared them. Most of the meetings were with Brother Dil's congregation of Indians, Sri Lankans, and Pakistanis, but we also ministered to a group of Filipinos. These were all very hungry souls who ate up the Word as the Bread of Life, and begged for more.

Meanwhile, Sister June was finding out that she still had another complication. Her visa was in the lost passport, and now that she would be a woman travelling alone, the company that had given the first letter of invitation was uncomfortable about sponsoring her. This was a Muslim nation with very strict laws and traditions. Eventually, someone was found who was willing to be responsible for her, and she was able to get her visa. She arrived a day or two before we left. All things working together for good, she was able to continue ministering to these dear people and provided good spiritual Bread to feed them.

It was a lesson that I have taken carefully to heart—don't engage a principality in spiritual warfare unless you have direct orders from Heaven to do so!

Into Publishing Again

Eventually, a building was built for Papa Jim that we called "The Hanger." His office was moved there from the old office that had been built as an extension to Sister Gwen and Papa

Jim's house in 1979. We were then able to move our office from the new room and bedroom we had been occupying into this larger space. We had been terribly cramped and just about worked in each other's way. Around that time, the Lord brought a trained accountant to us, and I was relieved of the position.

We had farmed out our *End-Time Handmaidens Magazine* to a typesetting company and published one since the fire. Before the fire we were doing all of that in-house. My Dutch blood made me want to see us get back into doing it all ourselves, so we purchased the computer program we needed and got started with publishing again.

I did most of the typesetting and layout for our *Magazines* and some of our books. I helped to proofread and edit some of Sister Gwen's books through the years. I loved it! It was a creative vent for me.

More Travelling with Heather

Heather attended Jasper Public School until she was in the fifth grade. Each year the teachers graciously allowed us to take her out for our annual spring trip to Pennsylvania and sometimes other meetings in the eastern states. They felt that travel provided an important aspect of education and Heather always managed to keep her grades up.

The school also worked with us the year she was in the second grade and Philip and I had the opportunity to sing in the international choir at the Christian Celebration During the Feast of Tabernacles sponsored by the International Christian Embassy, Jerusalem. It was a tremendous chance to get acquainted and worship with anointed singers and musicians from the nations. The rehearsals were long, but Heather did a pretty good job of keeping up with her school work and had some fun times too. By this time she was already dancing in the conventions and events with the other young girls, so we brought along her long white dancing dress, just in case they needed her.

The relationships we formed in that time continue today. We can look forward to worshipping together for all eternity!

An Overdose of the Holy Ghost

When we began hearing in the early 1990's about "The Laughing Revival," we couldn't believe that it could possibly be from God. We were intercessors that wept before God for the concerns of His Kingdom and the degradation of the earth and the soon-coming time of trouble. Evidently we had forgotten our own experiences of Holy Laughter at times when we were overcome by the Holy Spirit, or that on the Day of Pentecost when the Holy Spirit was first poured out, the disciples were accused of being drunk with new wine.

Jim and Francine Lovell were always keeping their ear to the ground for the latest thing that God was doing, so they went to Rodney Howard-Brown's camp meeting. They brought back video tapes of the meetings, so we watched them in our devotions. The more we watched, the more we were convinced that it was the real thing. We became convinced that this was God when pastors were being interviewed and were virtually speechless. They would try to talk, but were so overcome by the power of God that they were unable to put more than two or three words together. Sister Gwen said, "Anytime a preacher can't talk, it's got to be God!"

Then I began to receive. I could feel the weight of the Glory of God penetrating me and taking me into a new place in the spirit realm. From that time on for months, the Holy Spirit would overpower me without warning and I was very likely to collapse on the floor.

Then we heard that the Holy Spirit was moving in Toronto. Sister Gwen heard about a conference that they were holding, so she and Papa Jim joined Francine and Jim, and went to check it out. When she saw that the worship leader had an earring and holes in his blue jeans, Sister Gwen was pretty sure this couldn't be the real thing, but when he started to sing beautiful songs that lined up with the scriptures, she gave up her negative thinking. Then she realized that this move in Toronto had started exactly fifty years after the outpouring that she had experienced in her Toronto Bible school!

Sometime later, we discovered that she herself had prophesied under a powerful anointing that God would pour out His Spirit in a mighty way on the City of York, which she found out later was the early name for Toronto.

About six months later, a delegation of five (Bill and Valerie Devlin, Shirley Elenbaas, Marylois and I) were sent to Toronto to learn how they minister this anointing using ministry teams. Before the training session, however, we experienced a meeting. Shirley had been there before, so she coached us a bit.

We were sitting very near the front, in about the second or third row, as hungry seekers do. When the message was over and the call for ministry given, there were no clear instructions about where to go and what to do. I didn't see anyone filling the altar area to be prayed for by the speaker, and since my back was to the rest of the crowd, I didn't see that all the seekers had gone to the back of the auditorium to stand on tape lines to wait their turn for a ministry team member to pray for them.

So I just stood there listening to the anointed music and closed my eyes, worshipping. After a while, I heard in my spirit, "Come away, My beloved!" I wasn't sure what I was supposed to do, but decided to take a few steps forward. I saw that there was some activity going on to the right of the platform, so I went that direction. By this time Bob, the worship leader had moved off the platform (his guitar and microphone were wireless), and so had the lady violinist. When I spotted them, the Holy Spirit came over me and I froze in midstride. They both saw what had happened to me and moved my direction, all the while continuing the music. The next thing I knew, I was bending over and they each extended a knee in front of me as I heaved forward. Now I knew all about the laying on of hands, but I had never heard of laying of knees! That's another incident that I want to follow up on when I get to the video replay department in Heaven. I know that I received some kind of an impartation in the worship realm, but I would like to know more about what happened from God's point of view!

After that encounter was over, I walked a bit further around the back of the platform and the Holy Spirit overwhelmed me again. This time I collapsed on the floor in a fetal position and began weeping with great heaving sobs. Before long, one of the ministry team ladies knelt down beside me and began to pray for me. She discerned the cause of my deep agony of soul and told me that this was a very deep wound and wouldn't be healed instantly. She said that in six weeks time, I would find that it was mended.

For the next weeks it was as though I had amnesia about the incident, but when six weeks had passed, I suddenly remembered it. I realized that it didn't hurt anymore. I remembered what had caused my pain, but the memory didn't make me cry as it had before—it simply didn't hurt! Glory to God!

For the next year or two, I was still subject to being overcome by the Holy Spirit and collapse or appear to be drunk or be speechless, but then someone prayed for me to have structure in my spirit to be able to hold up and carry the anointing to pour it out on others. I am seldom overcome like that anymore.

More Nations: Tibet

When Sister Gwen was in India in 1966, while working in the Himalayas, she began to have a burden for Tibet and prayed much for that closed, forbidden land. She had her "Who Is Jesus?" tract translated into Tibetan for the thousands of refugees from there that were living in the area. Then she and Papa Jim were able to go there on a commercial tour in 1981, shortly after China opened it to tourism.

We were able to get a Bible in the Tibetan language and reproduce the Gospels of Mark and John for workers that were going there.

Then the Lord put it on Sister Gwen's heart to send a small tour group in 1993 to redeem the land there and pray. She chose Philip and me to lead the group. As we prayed about it, we felt that we had a mandate from the Lord to "build a beachhead in the spirit realm by praise and worship." The Lord put the group together and it was amazing how beautifully we sounded together. We asked the tour guide as he was showing us around the various temples and monasteries, to let us know when we arrived at the highest point where we would go in each building or mountain pass. When he told us, we would break into song, praising and worshipping the Lord. It was like holes were being punched in the spiritual atmosphere.

That is not to say that it was easy. It was the most intensely dark place we had ever experienced and we met a great deal of resistance, with two or three of our team coming under tremendous attack. Thankfully, we knew that we did not have a mandate to take on any principalities, but we sang and worshipped the Lord Most High in the midst of the idolatry and demonic activity. We kept short accounts, meeting together each morning for devotions and Holy Communion, and again at the end of the day to debrief. It was a wonderful team that flowed together in unity in such a beautiful way.

I was still wearing my hair in a braid across the top of my head at that time. There was mutual delight to discover that my style was typical of most of the Tibetan ladies. I could hear them twittering and giggling as they pointed at my head. I was full of wonder at the goodness of the Lord to put such a simple thing as that in my heart, and that He could use it to help open the hearts of the people to us and what the Holy Spirit was doing through us.

Part of me wanted to go back and part never wanted to get around that much darkness again. At the World Convention in 1999, some of the Tibet group gathered and begged us to take them back. Philip and I backpeddled as hard as we could, but agreed to pray about it. We asked the Lord to make His will clear to us.

That summer, we accompanied Sister Gwen and Papa Jim, along with Cola and Heather, on a ministry tour in the Pacific Northwest, arranged by ETH Betty Graves. After ministering in Ontario, Oregon, we took off on a journey all around the states of Oregon and Washington. On one leg of the journey, Sister Gwen decided that we needed to get off the highway and find ice cream (she loved it). As we drove through the nearest town in search of the frozen delight, we drove past a Tibetan Furniture store. Philip and I looked at each other and wondered if God might be trying to tell us something. One of the homes we stayed in had a coffee table book about the Tibetans in Ladakh. Again we looked at each other. Then when we arrived at the church pastored by Sister Gwen's cousin, Les Bergman. He and his wife, Ellen, invited us to go to the sanctuary to pray in preparation for the service. There on the altar was a Tibetan flag! And as if that weren't enough, Ellen brought out some little booklets and asked, do these look familiar? "Yes," I exclaimed, "we printed them!" They were the Gospel portions in Tibetan.

When we arrived home, Philip received a catalog from one of the companies from which he buys parts for our 1984 Toyota Land Cruiser. On the cover was a car identical to ours. The caption said that it was crossing the Nepal Tibet border! Okay! Okay! We get the message!

To ice the cake, a couple months later, Sister Gwen walked into my office with a calendar and handed it to me saying, "Here's another prophetic sign." It said, "Tibet 2000" on it with fantastic photos of the land and people. We began to make plans for a tour!

I was able to go to India again in February of 2000, with Glenn and Charlen Logemann. Due to the altitude of the Himalayas, it was very cold and I wore many layers to stay warm. I was very grateful for every cup of hot tea, and my hot water bottle! We drove several places, visiting with and ministering to the End-Time Handmaidens and Servants. One day we went to the border of Tibet to pray.

I began to get a plan for the trip for later in the year. The last time we had gone, we flew in, drove around and flew back to Kathmandu. This time, I felt we should fly in and drive back out—when we arrived, we found that the cars we used were very similar to ours, and when we arrived at the hotel in Lhasa, one exactly like ours was parked in front—what a welcome!

Some of the same team members were with us this second time and some new ones, but we felt the assignment was the same. This time we went into a lot of new territory we hadn't been able to cover previously. We had a tremendous time of worship at over 17,000 feet (over 5,181 meters) on the highest mountain pass we crossed, with gale winds whipping at us.

Although there was still a darkness in the place, knowing that many, many prayer groups had visited in the years in between, it felt more like the darkness was now a façade, like the background sets on a stage that provide the visual setting for a play. We were thrilled at the progress that the Kingdom of God had made, and knew that it was just a matter of time before the kingdom of darkness would collapse like a house of cards.

South Africa

I attended three or four of the South African End-Time Handmaidens and Servants Conventions. I helped to lead the worship at one and spoke at two of them. Once we brought a

The local people loved to sing and dance along when we praised the Lord.

Daily Holy Communion was essential to keep us focused on the Lord and His purposes for us to be in Tibet.

We worshipped the Lord in the high places to make a "beachhead" for His soon return.

tour group and went as well to Kwazulu-Natal to minister at a convention, and then took the group to Kruger National Park to experience a safari. We enjoyed seeing lions, cheetahs, giraffes, zebras, all manner of antelope species, rhinos, Cape buffalo, elephants, and many more types of animals.

Another time, I led a group of eight ladies and we redeemed the waters at Cape Agulhas, the southernmost tip of Africa, where the Indian Ocean meets the Atlantic. I had such a heavy burden from the Holy Spirit and travailed deeply over the land before we even arrived at the Oceans. It is a very dangerous, rocky coastline, and difficult to actually get to the water. I carefully clambered down the rocks to the point where I could just barely touch the waters. (Our host told me later that he thought he might have to dash out and rescue me if a wave suddenly carried me away.)

When we felt the Holy Spirit's "Amen," that the task was complete, I turned to come back up from my position. One of the ladies said, "Wait! We need a picture of this!" I started to react religiously and fuss at her for thinking of something so carnal at such a spiritual moment, but the Lord breathed His grace on me. To strike a pose, I turned and held my shofar up to my lips to give one last mighty sound to conclude our activity, while she snapped the photo. Now you have to know that my shofar has a menorah carved in it, and in that instant, the sun lined up with the central or "servant" candle position. Then I remembered that someone had had a vision that was turned into a banner used at the South African Convention: A Menorah stood at the southernmost tip of Africa and the "servant" candle lit a revival fire that burned all the way up the continent! Glory to God!

Another time Philip and Heather and I were able to go to South Africa together. I was invited to teach in a YWAM affiliate school in Pretoria. The school focused on helping people from different cultures redeem their redeemable cultural activities

Visiting a wigwam in Virginia

Recording the "Song for Kayla"

Heather's first day of school.
The dog had chewed on her
shoe the day before!

We visited a private game park in Zimbabwe.
The lion cub is heavy!

to offer to God in praise and worship. One weakness in the history of missions is that the missionaries carried not only the Gospel, but also Western culture. We saw it ourselves in Cuba, where all the men came to church, went to the room beside the platform, borrowed a tie to wear, then went to sit down with the congregation, as though wearing a tie were an important ritual in the Bible.

I taught them about the shofar and some of them could relate it to using the conch shell in their culture. We taught the principles of redeeming the land and many other principles from the Word of God.

Zimbabwe

From South Africa, Philip, Heather and I flew to Harare, Zimbabwe. We were met by Denis and Joan Cooper and taken to their farm/retreat centre called, Shiloh Shalom. We had an End-Time Handmaidens and Servants Retreat and the power of God was greatly manifest.

Afterwards, our dear friend and former Engeltal staff member, Issy Staunton took us on a wonderful journey to Rusitu Mission near Chipinge. I wanted to go there to the place where Rees Howells, the great intercessor, had seen such revival, signs and wonders. We could only be there overnight, but put up our tent in the abandoned chapel where the Holy Spirit had been outpoured. The roof had been demolished during the war with nearby Mozambique, and it had never been repaired. What a wonderful experience we had in the Presence of the Lord that night, just taking in a bit of the atmosphere and tapping into the glory deposit that still lingers there.

Rebuilding Our Offices

In the meantime, work had been going on in Engeltal to rebuild our office building. ETH&S Alouise and Wayne Berry came to stay with us for a good while, and Wayne helped oversee the building process of what we call "The Ark." We moved in on March 17, 1995, exactly four years and four months after Qumran burned to the ground.

We had a praise march around the building and a dedication service in the new classroom called "Torah Hall."

The day before the fire, Don Thompson gave Papa Jim a check to help pay for a sprinkler system to be installed in Qumran. He felt there was danger of fire. His check burned that night. Of course the Lord has seen to it that the Ark is better than Qumran in many ways—and it does have a sprinkler system!

Argentina Team without Sister Gwen

In 1997, Linda Hartzell planned a trip to Argentina that would have a large team to accompany Sister Gwen having large meetings in major cities and smaller meetings for smaller parts of the team. Sister Gwen and Papa Jim were staying in Israel after the tour just to have a vacation. They spent some days at the Dead Sea and were exposed to someone with bronchitis. She came down with it and then got on the plane to fly to Toronto where they were scheduled to change flights and meet us in Miami to fly together to Argentina. Much to our dismay, when she arrived in Toronto, she was so sick that she saw a doctor at the airport and he grounded her. She was forced to cancel her trip, but all the rest of us were already en route to Miami. She told us, "You girls will have to just do it without me. It's the same Holy Ghost whether I'm there or not."

So Linda and I gulped hard and agreed. What else could we do? In city after city we preached and the team helped too. We were just trying to follow the leading of the Holy Spirit. When we reached Córdoba, we found huge crowds of thousands coming to the meetings. The Lord was faithful and ministered through us. The final night I was planning to teach out of one of Sister

Gwen's Bible studies. Brother Marcos said to me, "If Sister Gwen were here, she would be prophesying!" It was a direct challenge to me. I knew that I couldn't make anything up, but thus far in the meetings, the Holy Spirit hadn't moved me in that way. When I stepped up to the pulpit, a mighty anointing hit me and I prophesied for several minutes about the nation and the move that the Lord was going to bring in the Catholic Church. A shock wave went through the crowd. The Catholic Church had been persecuting the Evangelical Church for as long as these people had known, and they weren't very excited about their enemies receiving a move of God at first. But the Lord did exactly that, and the barriers have been breaking down ever since.

Thrust into Jerusalem

During our spring trip to the eastern states, Sister Gwen and Papa Jim were in the van with Philip and me as we were pulling on to the Garden State Parkway. Sister Gwen suddenly said, "What does 'thrust' mean?"

Philip and Papa Jim offered explanations about pushing and how a rocket is propelled upward by thrust.

Then she said, "The Lord just spoke to me and said, 'I am going to thrust you into Jerusalem.'"

A few months later, the second to last night of our ISOM, Rev. Derek Kuhn was teaching under a mighty anointing. He said that End-Time Handmaidnes have a very special end-time assignment in Israel, and particularly in Jerusalem. The Lord began to speak that we have a portion in Israel.

Brother Derek said, "I want to give the first thousand dollars to this project." And Brother Doorn piped up that he had wanted to give the first thousand, but Derek beat him to it!

Sister Gwen didn't want to accept this added burden and responsibility, and said, "I'm not taking an offering!" However,

God took the control of it as one after another stood up to donate or pledge monthly. She left the platform and sat down. We received $7,000 in gifts immediately, and altogether over $45,000 in pledges.

He began to remind Sister Gwen of how some years earlier, He had commissioned ETH Naphtali to intercede at the Western Wall in Jerusalem. Every night for some years she prayed there from midnight to six a.m. God said that through her faithful intercession she had "purchased" for us an inheritance in Israel. Just like God gave Rahab, Ruth, and Obed-Edom, an inheritance, even though they were not Israelites.

Later I reminded her how God had spoken to her while we were driving on to Garden State Parkway. She was also encouraged by one of the dictionary examples of "thrust" that says, "They thrust extra responsibilities on her." It helped her grasp that she didn't have much choice in this matter.

We felt the Lord would have us call it the House of Peace. It took a while to find it, but by faith we kept collecting funds for its purchase. The Lord gave Sister Gwen the scripture about how Jesus sent the disciples to prepare their final Passover meal with Him. He told them that they would meet a man carrying a water pot and he would lead them to an upper room that was furnished and ready for them (Luke 22:10-12).

Imagine her amazement when the real estate agent, Emunah, led her to this place on the third floor and at the door were beautiful, clay water pots decorating the entrance! The place was being sold with all the furnishings, and amazingly, the owners were a Jewish couple from the United States who understood U.S. real estate practices and agreed to allow us to purchase it on a three-year contract, instead of the complicated process that the Israelis typically use. By the miracle of God and the generosity of our givers, we were able to pay it off in two years!

Angelo

One of the books that has influenced me deeply was Rick Joyner's, *The Final Quest*. The entire book has given me wisdom to recognize the hand of God in situations where I needed guidance.

Perhaps the most helpful part of all was near the end where Rick is in Heaven, having the privilege of experiencing the judgment of God now so that he could go back to earth and make some corrections in his life and attitudes. There he met a "king" named Angelo. I won't go into the whole story, but suffice it to say that in his earthly life, Angelo had been a deaf street person who loved the Lord, but Rick had rejected him. As a child, he had been locked in a closet, and when found was turned over to the foster care system where he suffered more abuse.

The Lord had first shown him to Rick in a vision many years before. He saw two men, one a fine upstanding Christian family man, the other was Angelo, a vagrant walking through a park, who angrily shoved a kitten aside with his foot. Jesus asked Rick, "Which of these men please me more?"

Rick's reply was what most of us would have said, "The first man."

"No," was the answer. "That man was given 100 portions of love and he's only using 75 of them. Angelo was only given one portion of love and he used all of it to keep from killing the kitten." The Lord rewarded him by giving him three more portions of love. Each time he used them fully, the Lord would give him some more. He was an overcomer, empowered by the love of God.

That story had helped me look to the Lord more in forming my attitudes about people. We don't know how many portions of love were given to people, or how fully they are using what

I've always enjoyed advertising books

Heather and Kiwi

It was a privilege to have Philip's mother, Dorothy with us in Niagara Falls at Rainbow House.

I set up my little office in our bedroom at Rainbow House.

While stationed at Rainbow House, we returned to Engeltal to help with events.

they've been given. We have to tune in to the Lord to get His viewpoint — it's the only one that has any value.

Sister Gwen wrote a tremendous sermon booklet on the principle of *Knowing One Another in the Spirit*. It will also help you to get God's perspective on His people.

I remember one time there was a gal that came to the World Conventions and made quite a spectacle of herself. She wasn't pretty, and it was obvious that she wasn't mentally very sharp. She loved the Lord, though, and fasted 21 days. When Sister Gwen was presented with her application for approval, she wanted to reject her as being an embarrassment to the ministry. The Lord spoke to her, "If I don't reject her, how can you?" The lady took her vows that convention.

I try to walk softly with regard to people. I remember seeing a poster once that said, "People are fragile. Handle with care." I try to remember that "Mercy triumphs over judgment" (James 2:13 NKJV). When you are dealing with difficult people, it is sometimes necessary to take a stand, but it can be done in love. We need to learn to administer correction without rejection.

"He's My Son!"

I was concerned once about a man I had met, thinking that he had some certain sin in his life. I began praying about it, perhaps out of nosiness. I was asking the Lord if what I was suspecting about him were true. Then I heard His Voice so clearly in my spirit say, "He's My son!"

Well, that was the end of my offensive inquisitiveness! I realized that, first of all, it was none of my business, and secondly, God was overseeing the man as His own son. We need to be careful not to give any place to the accuser of the brethren!

141

Taking Out the Stress

One time when we went to church with my sister Chris, the minister shared a story that has stuck with me through the years. It was about a young man who was dating the girl he loved, but was frustrated with her perpetual habit of tardiness. He decided to "cure" her by promising to take her to some event she really wanted to go to, but she had to promise to be ready half an hour early, or he would tear up the tickets. She agreed.

When he arrived to pick her up, her mother shook her head sadly and said that it would be impossible for her to be ready on time since she had only come in five minutes earlier.

The young man fumed as he waited for her in her father's study. He was trying to decide whether to tear up the tickets or not. So the young man asked her father how it was that he and the girl's mother had such a wonderful marriage. The man said that he tried to live by this simple rule:

> For every evil under the sun,
> There is a remedy, or there is none;
> If there be one, search 'til you find it,
> If there be none, never mind it.

The young man was set free from his need to control his girlfriend's tardiness and just learn to live with something he couldn't change when he made her his wife.

When I come to a situation that I cannot change, the Holy Spirit reminds me of this poem. It helps take the stress out of life. I'm convinced that frustration is caused by our inability to control a situation, but the truth of the matter is, God is ultimately in control so we don't need to feel that we have to be.

Stationed at Rainbow House of Prayer

When Heather turned 18 in the middle of her senior year in high school, we felt the Lord would have us go to our Rainbow House of Prayer in Niagara Falls for a while. When Sister Gwen was asked how long this would be, she said, "I don't know, a week, two weeks, maybe a year." In the end it was about three weeks longer than a year. We did a lot of fixing up and painting, as well as keeping worship and intercession going. We held a weekly worship and Bible study meeting, and hosted retreats. We were blessed to be able to go across the border into Canada to minister a number of times, all in accordance with the original vision for Rainbow House. I remember once in worship that I became aware of something like Jacob's ladder in the room. Every time I've been there since, I sense that it is there.

Mother-Daughter Cruise

Presidents' Day weekend in February, 2007, Sister Gwen was invited to be a speaker for a Mother-Daughter Cruise. She invited all the staff ladies to come along. I left Rainbow House for what I thought would be the weekend. Heather was able to take a day or two off from classes at IHOP and came along. It was wonderful to be with her again for a few days without a lot of responsibilities. I helped with some of the music for the meetings, but it was mostly a restful time.

Papa Jim hadn't been quite himself and couldn't really retain where we were or what we were doing. We ate our meals together and sometimes he seemed quite lucid and other times not. By the end of the cruise, he was acting strangely and fell out of bed in the night several times.

Sister Gwen had been scheduled to speak in a number of meetings around Florida. She realized that she needed to take Papa Jim home and see a doctor. She asked me to step in for her and take those meetings, which I did.

Becoming Vice President

Papa Jim was diagnosed with masses on his brain (two of them inoperable), and it became obvious that he was not going to be with us for long. He told Sister Gwen that he was ready to go home to Heaven. He was only with us for about two and a half weeks from that point and spent his last days in the nursing home in Jasper, about seven miles from Engeltal. Sister Gwen and I had one very small, brief window of time when the two of us were alone there in the room with Papa Jim. She turned to me and she pointed her finger at me and said "You're my VP," and I knew what that meant.

Some years earlier, when Sister Gwen, Papa Jim, and Philip and I stayed over in Jerusalem after the Israel Tour group went home, Gene and Marylois took us on an excursion to Galilee. We were sitting in the VW van and Sister Gwen turned to me and said, "You can have my mantle if you are with me when I go." For years I was nervous when I was away on ministry trips when she was ill, that she might leave while I was gone. Then more recently she said to me, "You don't actually have to be present in the room, you just have to be 'with me.' Do you understand?" That set me a bit freer, because I truly was "with her" all the way, but I still wanted to be there for her in her last days.

I can't tell you how many people through the years—intercessors and prophets—whispered or declared to me that I would take Sister Gwen's mantle or her office or her work when the Lord takes her home. I just thanked them, knowing what the Lord had spoken to me all those years earlier.

But when Sister Gwen said, "You're my VP," I realized that there actually was a reality in the word I had heard in my spirit in 1976, and that all these prophetic voices were also right. I had laid aside the whole idea, not really knowing if it were true. A number of times through the years I had faced discouragement and was tempted to leave Engeltal, but I wondered, "Where would I go?"

At that point I would remember Jesus' question to His disciples when many people became offended with His words and left Him. He asked them, "Will you also go away?"

Peter responded, "Lord, to whom shall we go? Thou hast the words of eternal life" (John 6:68).

There was no other ministry that I knew that caused my spirit to resonate like this one. Sister Gwen had "the words of life" for me. The accuser of the brethren would taunt me that it wasn't God that spoke to me and I should just give it up. I concluded that it didn't matter if it was God or not that spoke to my spirit; I was where I was supposed to be. I was helping Sister Gwen in her ministry, and the Lord was using her to change lives and bring them closer to Himself. I wasn't wasting my time!

The time came to have a Board meeting to elect the officers and replace the other board members. That is when I officially became the Vice President/Treasurer and Philip became the Secretary. We actually needed two board members, because Dorothy Buss was not able to hold her office anymore. So that is when we brought Brother Emmanuel Jibuike and Doris Swartz onto the Board of Directors. I was so happy to have both of them on the Board as they had both taken the leadership of their organizations following the passing of prominent dignitaries. I wanted them to be with us for the transition that I knew would be coming eventually.

I remember leaving that meeting and walking along the sidewalk. All of a sudden, the enormity of what had just taken place began to hit me. I had just been elected the Vice-President/Treasurer, of the End-Time Handmaidens and Servants International. It was really overwhelming!

As a great weight of responsibility seemed to be loading me down, I suddenly had a vision, of something that looked like a PVC pipe about five inches in diameter and about thirty feet long. It was suspended about six inches above my shoulders. I pondered that for a moment, then saw that on either side of me was an angel. The angels were carrying this yoke with their arms extended down in a relaxed manner at their sides. Even though I didn't see them in their full height, I could estimate that if their arms were at full length and their hands were holding the "pipe" six inches above my shoulders, they were pretty big—maybe eleven feet tall. Then the revelation dawned on me. I realized that my job was just to stay under the yoke. I don't have to carry it. If I only have to stay under it, I think I can do this!

The Busy Little Girl

During one of our devotions times in 2007, I had a vision of a little girl in a motorized, brightly-coloured, plastic kiddy car, in front of Bethlehem, our dining hall. She was driving furiously, moving the gear shift lever up and down, turning the wheel from side to side, but never going faster than the speed that had been preset by her daddy. I knew the little girl was me—always busy, always working so hard, but rarely taking time to be still—and never being able to break through beyond the speed of slow.

Sometime later, I had another vision of the same little girl. This time she was coming out of Bethlehem on a gurney, as still as she could be. Angels were moving her from the building to a silver limousine that was waiting outside. The door was open and I could see the cream-coloured leather interior. Golden light was pouring out from the inside of the car. I could see from this vision that the key to getting where I really wanted to go was to get out of the driver's seat and stop my frenetic pace, just trusting the Lord to take me to His destination.

We Almost Lost Sister Gwen

In March of 2008, one year after Papa Jim passed on, Sister Gwen, who had been in deep mourning all that time, became ill with influenza and pneumonia. We did not know the seriousness of it, but were very concerned. One evening at supper, I received a call to come quickly to her house. She was fading fast. I threw off my coat as I entered the room and strode towards her, rebuking the spirit of death. In short order, she began to come around, and was talking lucidly again.

We discussed taking her to the hospital to which she vehemently objected. So we put her to bed and kissed her good night.

The next evening, on Papa Jim's *jahrzeit*,[13] she worsened. We called her son, Tommy, to step in and make the decision to take her to the hospital. When we arrived at the Emergency Room, the nurses and doctors scrambled to get her to intensive care. They told us that she wouldn't have lasted much longer if we hadn't brought her in.

I knew that this was not her appointed time and was not worried, although the situation did not look good at all. At the end of her hospital stay, she took up her pen and notebook and began to write her last daily devotional, *He sent Me Back to Tell You.*

We Lost Dorothy

Philip's mother, Dorothy Buss, was living in a nursing home since we brought her back from Niagara Falls in November of 2006. She was near her eldest son, Scott, and his wife Carolyn, and her middle son, Gary, and his wife, Kristine were not very

13 *Jahrzeit,* a Judæo-German term, is the anniversary of a person's death.

far away. She was able to see most of her grandchildren and great-grandchildren from time to time while living there.

She entertained the residents with her piano playing and was able to attend concerts at Scot and Carolyn's school, Institute of Music, Worship, and the Arts.

While Sister Gwen was still in intensive care, we received word that Dorothy was sick with the flu. Sister Gwen graciously loaned me her car and I made a quick trip over to see Dorothy. That night we started our ISOM session without Sister Gwen. ETH Flo Ellers graciously stepped in for Sister Gwen, and Chuck and Mary Ann Flynn, June Lewis, and Rona Spiropoulos carried their teaching beautifully. It was a highly anointed school!

At the end of the first night's class, Philip and I were talking about whether he should go and see his mother when we got word that she had already passed on. It was as though the death angel had not been permitted to take Sister Gwen, so he went over and took Dorothy instead.

Her precious husband, Estel, had gone home to be with the Lord in 1993. The night he passed, I began to grieve deeply, expecting that the rest of the family would be experiencing the same depth of grief. They had to pray the spirit of grief off of me, and I have to say that I have never grieved that deeply since, thank God! I believe it was a remnant of the ache of missing my mom all those years, and God healed it, praise His wonderful Name!

Taking Her Place Began

Sister Gwen was very serious about keeping her commitments. Once she committed to preach for a small camp meeting in a remote location. Then she received an invitation to go to a nation she loved with a prominent minister. She struggled with the controversy in her own heart, but knew that she had to fulfil her commitment.

Her sense of commitment was so strong, that she did not want to leave an appointment unmet, so she would send someone else in her place, If the ministry would receive that one.

She had a season during which she was diagnosed with osteoporosis, and had two or three occasions when she suffered broken bones. On these occasions she sent me to take her place, and the Holy Spirit was faithful to do His work in the people.

Heather Marries

After Heather graduated from Jasper High School in 2006, she felt the Lord calling her to the Forerunner School of Music at the International House of Prayer (IHOP) in Kansas City. During that time, Philip and I were stationed at the End-Time Handmaidens Rainbow House of Prayer in Niagara Falls, New York. When Christmas came, Heather didn't want to go home to Engeltal since we weren't there, and she didn't really want to join us in Niagara Falls. She had so bonded with her new friends that it was on her heart to cook Christmas dinner for those who were still there.

When dinner time came, she wasn't ready, so her friends went back to the prayer room to get in some more time there. Meanwhile, Timm Saller, a friend of a friend that Heather had invited, knocked on the door of the house she shared with three other girls. She called, "Come in."

Now Timm had just been on a time of two weeks of fasting in seclusion with the Lord, seeking His face. One of the subjects he had been praying about was, "Lord, when are you going to send me my wife?"

TAKE THE LID OFF

The Buss Family at Heather and Timm's wedding

The Cooper Family at Heather and Timm's wedding

Just ten days after the wedding we were in an accident

Note how narrow the median was.

Through the kindness of my brother-in-law we were able to stay at Myers Lake Camp. We were led by still waters.

From the front door of Heather's house, you could look past the living room to the right and straight into the kitchen. The stove was right at the kitchen door and Heather was standing there stirring her mashed potatoes. He fell flat in love with her in that moment!

They were engaged the following Christmas in our home and married May 17, 2008. It was a splendid outdoor wedding in Engeltal, and the weather was perfect. Our Barbara Noyes put together an amazing array of food with the help of some of our Engeltal ladies, and Mannah Schmidt made the cake. It was beautiful. We will be forever grateful for all their help in making the day delightful!

The Accident

Just days after the wedding, Philip and I started out on a tour of our ETH&S Branches that would allow us to be in Michigan to celebrate my dad's 80th birthday before ending in New York. From there we were scheduled to fly to Israel to help lead the worship for an event being held on the Mount of Olives, sponsored by Sadhu Sundar Selverage/Jesus Ministries.

On Tuesday, May 27, 2008, on our way to Grand Rapids, Michigan, Philip was tired and asked me to drive. It was about 5:30 in the afternoon and traffic was moderately heavy. We were on I-94 in the middle of three lanes of traffic, just beginning to pass an eighteen-wheeler transport truck. Suddenly, while we were beside his rear wheels, the trucker put on his turn signal and began to move into our lane. Just as I was about to react, Philip woke up and shouted. "Sharon, the truck—he's coming over!" Instead of reacting to the situation by putting on the brake, and checking my mirrors, I reacted to the panic in his voice and pulled to the left, only to find a car in that lane. I pulled back to the right and found the truck still coming at us. Then I pulled left again and the car in the left lane had wisely sped up out of the way.

As we headed for the narrow median, still going 70 miles an hour (112 kilometers), I remembered a story that Sister Gwen had told about going out of control on ice and heading for the median. She took her hands off the steering wheel and called out, "Jesus!" knowing that putting herself in His hands was safer than trying to control it herself.

So that's what I did—I took my hands off the wheel and put my trust in the Lord, "Jesus," I shouted. And Philip also called out, "Jesus!" Then I heard and felt the tremendous, "Whump!" of our first impact, having gone end over end. The shouting and "whumping" continued for two or three more impacts as we spun in the air, and the vehicle finally came to rest on it's side.

During the seconds for all this to take place, I heard inside me, "That window beside you is probably broken. You'd better pull your hand in." So I did.

Philip blacked out at the first impact, but continued to call out Jesus' name.

Suddenly all was still. I was dangling in my seat, held in by the seat belt. I looked at Philip, lying so still below me. His right hand was out the broken window on the pavement, the nail of his index finger on his left hand was floating, and I could see some blood on his head. My first thought was, "Dear Lord, have I just killed my husband?" I spit out some glass and said, "Honey, are you all right?"

He spit out some glass and said, "Yeah."

Then I assessed my own injuries. My right wrist had apparently slammed against the steering wheel while we tumbled, and rebounded, slinging my hand up along the sharp corner of the cup holder. The entire back of my hand was sliced open. I grabbed it and held on to stop the bleeding, and asked, "Are you really all right?"

"I don't think so," he groaned. Then he looked up at me and said, "Don't unbuckle your seat belt. Remember Betty Hill."

Betty's story had already crossed my mind and I had reached the same conclusion not to release my seat belt. Betty, Heather's first nanny, had told us the story of her own roll-over experience. The car had landed upside down and when she evaluated herself for injuries, she was happy to find she wasn't hurt. However, when she released her seat belt, she landed on her neck and suffered from it ever after.

By this time, "good Samaritans" came running, shouting to see if we were all right and to let us know that the ambulance was on the way. In a matter of minutes, the ambulance had arrived. The attendant showed me where to set my foot so that I could safely release the seat belt and not fall on Philip. They pulled back the broken windshield and helped me climb out. At first I thought that I was doing fine, but began to get light-headed, so I sat down on the pavement. Someone brought me my glasses, and then found my cell phone. I immediately called Engeltal to let everyone know to pray.

Having been on an ambulance team, I had an idea of what would be next. A cervical collar went around my neck and they got me ready to transport on a backboard. As they hoisted me up on the gurney, I thought about this being a new angle— being the patient instead of the EMT. Then I remembered the vision of the little girl on the gurney and wondered if I had come to that place.

The pain from the wrist injury was intense. It was all I could think about. I went through x-rays, etc. and found the only broken bone was a tuft fracture on the joint of my right thumb. The nurse tried to give me morphine and discovered I was allergic to it, so they used something else to relieve the pain. I was bruised in many places, but felt generally okay

Philip was another story, however. After x-rays and CT-scans, he was diagnosed with a tuft fracture on one finger and a torn tendon, two nails were badly damaged and one had to be sewed back on. There were multiple abrasions on his arm where it had been dragged across the pavement. His neck was badly hurt, but we didn't actually find out all the details until some months later. His spinal cord had been bruised, causing him to black out on our first tumble. This resulted in his neck and shoulder muscles being in a constant state of contraction without being able to relax.

At first I was sure that we were going to just continue on with our plans and go to Israel. ETH Inie DeJager picked us up and took us to her home, arriving about four or five in the morning. She put us to bed for a few hours, then I got up and went with her to the ETH Grand Rapids Branch meeting. Philip didn't feel like going.

I was still running on adrenaline at that point, and ministered in the meeting dressed in the same clothes I had been wearing in the accident.

The next day we went to the totaled car and retrieved our stuff, and then we went to the accident site to collect what we could find. We found a number of our belongings, including my shofar that had been broken in two pieces.

We were stunned to see how narrow the median actually was. The evidence was there that the car had landed on the shoulder of the oncoming lanes, depositing the carrots from our cooler on the pavement. Then it had rolled back to land on the shoulder of the lanes we had left, depositing our cherry tomatoes there. We never went past the rumble strips on either side of the highway! Glory to God! It was like the angels had lined up and linked arms, standing on the rumble strips on both sides of the median to say, "This far and no farther!"

Pausing the Journey

Our next destination was Detroit. ETH Hedy Wilton met us halfway and took us to her home. Philip rested while I went to the meeting and ministered as best I could with my waning strength. The adrenaline was beginning to wear off.

By this time we knew that we couldn't go on to Israel. Neither of us could play our guitars and we didn't really feel like going anywhere.

Hedy took us to my sister, Chris,' house at Myers Lake United Methodist Campground, where her husband, Jon, is the director. They warmly received us, and let us settle in one of the houses on the campground, telling us we could stay as long as we needed to. As I walked into the bedroom, I saw the beautiful view of quiet, little Myers Lake, and I heard in my spirit, "He leadeth me beside the still waters" (Psalm 23:2).

Sunday was the day we were to celebrate Dad's birthday, so we went to church with him and had a cake and reception following the service. The accident had actually happened on his birthday. He told me later how sad he was to see us arriving in such pain, but he was so thankful to the Lord that we were alive!

We remained there in that beautiful, quiet place for five weeks until Philip was able to travel. Between us we had one good hand—my left one. At least I was able to write, as I'm left-handed. We were pretty miserable for a while, but were grateful for the love, care and help of family members. After about two or three weeks I found myself humming again and realized that I hadn't had a song in me for those weeks. I hum or whistle most of the time, or at least have a song going in my head.

That was one of the three years that we had a camp meeting at Engeltal instead of World Convention, and we got home around the fourth of July. I was grateful that we didn't have to pack up and move so much like we did for Convention. By that time I was able to play my guitar again, so we could still lead some of the song services. It took longer for Philip to get his guitar playing back, and even longer before he could travel.

Canada, Elkton, and Strawberry Lake

That summer I went with the team to our International Convention in Canada, leaving Philip home to convalesce. On the way there, we stopped at Enoch Farm in Elkton, South Dakota, to be in meetings with ETH&S Karen and Steve Nelson, Karen's sister, ETH Teresa Crevier, and others of the clan. We had a marvelous time in the Presence of the Lord.

The Convention was wonderful, too, with Sister Gwen's co-worker from her Hong Kong, India, Pakistan and first Russia trip, Alice Shevkenek. Georges Sada, former advisor to Saddam Hussein also spoke, telling what it was like under that dictator and what a great thing America did to oust him.

From there we went to Strawberry Lake as Gerald Derstine had invited Sister Gwen to minister there. We were blessed to be able to go and pray in the place where the Holy Spirit had been so mightily outpoured in 1954 and 1955. Scholars refer to this as the earliest beginning of the Charismatic movement. I love going back to places where the Holy Spirit has moved, to gather some threads to weave into my own tapestry of experience and to pray for God to do it again!

Nigeria

Apostle Emmanuel Jibuike, General Overseer of The True Church of God denomination in Nigeria, and member of our End-Time Handmaidens and Servants Board of Directors, invited me to come to his country to be a speaker at the ETHS

Nigeria Convention in 2009. Philip still wasn't able to travel, so I had to go without him. We had wonderful meetings and I also spoke at a couple of churches in Lagos, then went by bus to Abuja, the capital city.

In Abuja, we met with several Handmaidens and visited one of the senators who is a strong Believer. I also went with a group to do some redeeming of the land, teaching them as we went. As we drove across the city to various points for prayer, I noticed some strange birds flocking over a hill. When I commented about it, one of the men said, "Those are not birds, they're bats, and they are swarming over the presidential palace compound!" I was shocked in the heat and bright sunshine of midday, here were bats flying all around the area of the home of the head of state. Wow, that was creepy! I was told that a great deal of murder and cannibalism have taken place there, so that would explain why these denizens of darkness would feel at home there at midday!

We had some more meetings in the area, then flew back to Lagos. It was an amazing experience. I love Africa and its amazing people groups. We know that the Light of the Lord Jesus is transforming this Dark Continent into a home for His glorious Kingdom.

Israel

For a while, Sister Gwen didn't feel up to going to Israel for an annual tour, but we started again in 2010. That was Philip's first overseas journey since the accident.

Israel is God's time clock. You can tell where we are in His prophetic plan by watching what happens in Israel. Sister Gwen was always fascinated with the Land of Israel and how that in her lifetime, the modern nation was born and has grown and prospered. She used to tell of how her grandfather prophesied that the Jewish people

A wonderful welcoming committee met me at the airport in Lagos, Nigeria and treated my royally for my whole stay.

We had a glorious time in the Lord at the End-Time Handmaidens and Servants Grand Convocation

This photo, taken in Israel, shows the place on Philip's head that went gray after the fire. One sister said, "That's where God touched him on top of the head."

We had the privilege of planting trees in Israel in memory of Sister Gwen during our 2013 Hearts for Israel Tour.

would soon come back into their land, and how she saw scripture fulfilled in Hong Kong when she could purchase Jaffa oranges there (Isaiah 27:6).

The Lord used her to plant a great love in my heart for Israel and her people. Sometimes I begin to get tears in my eyes when I just see Hebrew script.

I am also passionate about the fact that God made His covenant with Abraham, Isaac, and Jacob at altars that were built in what the godless media and political "powers" call "The West Bank." It is indeed the western bank of the Jordan River, but it is the heartland of the Biblical Promised Land, known in the Bible as Judea and Samaria. No nation in the earth has the right to put it under any governing authority other than the descendants of Abraham, Isaac, and Jacob. It's God's Land (He said so), and He will dictate who will inhabit it.

It was so very eye-opening to us when we began to get acquainted with some of the so-called "settlers" who live in this region. Most of them are passionate believers in the God of their fathers, Abraham, Isaac, and Jacob. They have moved there to build cities, towns and villages, and have become farmers and vine dressers simply because the Bible commands them to do so.

Sometimes we took ETH&S tours and sometimes I went with our travel agent, Madeleine Cohen on her "Fam" (Pastors' Familiarization) Tours. We went there in the best of times and in the worst of times. I don't believe in cancelling unless the airplanes won't fly there. When Heather was turning fourteen, she and I went on a "Fam." This was during the second intifada when suicide bombers were rampant. We actually heard two or three of them detonate, but we never felt unsafe. It was during that time that I began to say, "You are safer in a war zone in the will of God than in your own bed out of the will of God." We were there as intercessors and did we pray! One afternoon on that tour, we stopped for lunch at a small hotel. In the ladies room a local Israeli said to me, "You are so brave to come at this time!"

I said, "We came because of Isaiah 40:1, "Comfort ye, comfort ye my people."

She began to weep and told me that her daughter had been on Ben Yehuda Street the night before, and left her friends just before the suicide bomber detonated himself (we had heard the explosion from our hotel). One of her friends was killed and now her daughter was suffering from "survivor's syndrome." This makes you question, "Why wasn't I the one that was killed," and makes you feel guilty for being alive. She was traumatized.

I took this total stranger in my arms and wept with her, praying for the Lord to comfort her heart and heal her daughter of the trauma. It was the highlight of my trip to know that my ordinary human arms, motivated by the compassion of the Lord could actually fulfil scripture, again making the Bible come alive.

Israel has excellent security and made short work of the suicide bomb threat. It is sad that it became necessary to build a security fence which in some places is a high concrete wall. There are Arab residents who suffer because of it, but if there had been no suicide bombers and other forms of terror tactics coming from their communities, the wall/fence wouldn't have been constructed.

I call them Arabs because that is what they called themselves until Yasser Arafat took the term to mean his people. Prior to Israel's declaration of statehood, it was the Jews who called themselves Palestinians. Many had lived there throughout the generations, but many whose forefathers had been driven away centuries earlier were returning to the Land God had promised them by eternal covenant.

When Heather turned sixteen, we were so blessed to be able to spend three months at the End-Time Handmaidens and Servants Galilee House. It was a special, and much-needed, family time for us before Heather left the nest. It was a bit of a challenge to run a bed and breakfast—and yes, I was the cook, but I loved helping people experience the Land. And I loved experiencing it for myself more as a temporary resident than a tourist. It was great to go to the *shuk* (open market) and shop for the lovely fruits and vegetables.

Each day we would have a time of worship and intercession; most of the time it was just the three of us. We cultivated a beautiful three-part harmony, taking turns with the melody. About once a month we hosted an event at the house and some of the neighboring Believers came to enjoy a time of worship and the Word.

What a privilege it has been to coordinate the Israel Tours for Sister Gwen and the End-Time Handmaidens and Servants. I quit counting how many times I have gone when I got to thirty. A couple of years ago, all through the tour I was grousing in my head, "I'm getting too old for this. I'm getting tired of this. I don't want to do this anymore. I don't think I want to do this next year."

Then on the last day while I was eating my lunch I heard that Voice in my spirit, "So why don't you think you should do another tour next year?" I've learned that when the Lord asks you a question, it's not because He doesn't know the answer! So I repented and got my attitude right. The next tour we had was phenomenal, and we are continuing to plan more. Look at our website for the next one.

Journaling

Sister Gwen first began writing daily devotional books in 1982 because she wanted to have a devotional book for the tour members on their pilgrimage in the Holy Land. She searched and searched without success, so she decided to write one herself. It is called, *Devotional Meditations for a Pilgrim.*

161

She wrote each morning in the Presence of the Lord and read it to us on the bus. When the tour was over and she went on to Egypt, she continued writing, so the book consists of thirty days of writings.

She was so enjoying the Lord speaking to her so clearly from various scriptures every morning, and she couldn't stop writing. Before she knew it, she had written a year's worth of devotionals, and published it as *Daily Preparations for Perfection*. Then she began writing from the Psalms and that became the book, *Day by Day*. She then began work on the books of Proverbs and Ecclesiastes, enough for two volumes. Sadly, the majority of that work was lost in the fire. After the fire, and after a period of mourning, the Lord began to speak to her again, this time from the "red letters," that is to say from His words recorded in the New Testament.

At some point in the late 1980's or 1990, she decided that it was time for all of her staff to begin writing like this. She put all of our names in a container and each morning in devotions, she would pull a name. That person then had to read the writing they had received from the Lord that morning. It was a great experience and made us realize that we can all hear from God that way if we will just get still enough and listen.

Through the years I have journaled off and on, and try to be sensitive when the Lord is speaking in my spirit to write it down. Following are a few excerpts that I had typed previously, some for my portion of our prayer letter. I hope they minister to you.

From My Journal:
The Magnet of Holiness

Holy, holy, holy! Lord, You are so Holy! Holiness exudes from You. The angels react and cry, Holy! Holy! Holy!

Lord Jesus, how did You do it—You Who are so holy—coming to this unholy world?

There is nothing imperfect in Me. I Am complete and totally separate from everything that is not holy. I am clean. When I touch something that is unclean, it does not make Me unclean, it makes the unclean clean.

Humbling Myself to lay aside the heavenly and to take on My earthly form did not change the level of My holiness. In My earthly body, I still remained holy and incorruptible. I had to in order to give Myself as the sacrifice for all the sin of fallen mankind.

It is My love for you and for all My creation that motivated Me. I Am Love and I Am Holy. Holiness separates and love draws near. It's like the two ends of a magnet in relation to another magnet. One end repels and will not join itself and the other end attracts and will not let go.

When you try to come to Me in your own self-righteous "holiness," My true holiness will repel you and you will not even get close. But if you come with honest repentance, confessing your weakness, My love and compassion for you become so overwhelming that I rush to you and bond My strength, righteousness and holiness to your weakness to provide what you lack.

Lord, that is so kind of You! ….I'm hearing in my spirit the song, "The Power of Your Love," especially the line: "the weaknesses I see in me will be stripped away by the power of Your love"!

It's amazing how the accuser makes us feel so slimed by our own weaknesses that we don't feel we can bring them to You. He tempts us to sin then accuses and torments us once we yield. We feel so unworthy of Your love that we don't come and repent. Holy Spirit, please come and help us!

My love can and will transform you. Practice My Presence and bask in My love....We'll work together on this.

From My Journal:
Love Keeps No Record of Wrongs

Love keeps no record of wrongs. If you want Me not to retain your wrongs, you must not retain in your memory the wrongs of others. If you want Me to cleanse you of your sins and shortcomings by My Blood, then you must use My Blood to wash away your record of the wrongs and offenses of others.

When you find yourself offended or just annoyed at the actions or words of a sister or brother, ask Me to forgive them and use that grace to forgive them yourself. Apply My Blood to the offense.

These offenses and petty annoyances are keeping you earthbound and from rising up to the next level that you want to achieve in Me. My Blood is liquid love and it covers the multitude of sins (1 Peter 4:8).

On occasion, the circumstances that take place in a day might make you feel as though you've been slashed to ribbons. On one such day, I wondered how I would be able to go to supper and lead in singing the Doxology before our prayer of blessing for the food. I knew that it was essential that I sing from my heart with genuine praise and worship: "Praise God from whom all blessings flow..." As I did, I was delighted to see in the spirit that the places where I felt I had been lashed had become openings for the glory of God that I was feeling on the inside as I praised, to shine through. It was like a torn tent with a lamp inside would leak light through every little shredded place when camping in the darkness.

Don't be afraid of being wounded. Be quick to forgive. When your cup is tipped, what is going to spill out? Will it be the Love of God that you are meditating on? Or will it be anger or hurt? Let the Blood of the Lamb that was slain wash you and then wash away the sins of others, for "Whose soever sins ye remit, they are remitted unto them; and whose soever sins ye retain, they are retained" (John 20:23). Let's allow the Lord to use us to be carriers of forgiveness and peace.

"Unto him that loved us, and washed us from our sins in his own blood, …to him be glory and dominion for ever and ever. Amen" (Revelation 1:5).

From My Journal:
The Vengeance of God

Journal Entry, January 10, 2007

Lately, Philip and I have been singing the song that has the chorus that goes, "This is the year of the favour of the Lord. This is the day of the vengeance of our God." How good it is that His favour lasts a whole year and His vengeance only lasts a day!

Isaiah 63:4 "For the day of vengeance is in mine heart, and the year of my redeemed is come."

Isaiah 61:2 "To proclaim the acceptable year of the LORD, and the day of vengeance of our God; to comfort all that mourn;"

Isaiah 34:8 "For it is the day of the LORD's vengeance, and the year of recompences for the controversy of Zion."

Isaiah 66:14 "And when ye see this, your heart shall rejoice, and your bones shall flourish like an herb: and the hand of the LORD shall be known toward his servants, and his indignation toward his enemies."

Malachi 4:1-3 "For, behold, the day cometh, that shall burn as an oven; and all the proud, yea, and all that do wickedly, shall be stubble: and the day that cometh shall burn them up, saith the LORD of hosts, that it shall leave them neither root nor branch. But unto you that fear my name shall the Sun of righteousness arise with healing in his wings; and ye shall go forth, and grow up as calves of the stall. And ye shall tread down the wicked; for they shall be ashes under the soles of your feet in the day that I shall do this, saith the LORD of hosts."

The day of My wrath and vengeance was the day of My Son's crucifixion. As He obediently went into the custody of the High Priest's guards and then into the hands of the Romans, He bore all My wrath on all sin as the great subsitutionary sacrifice—the Lamb of lambs—the Lamb of God. His slaying was determined before the foundation of the world (Rev. 13:8), before sin existed, so that the justice would be total and complete for all time. Every sin was paid for at that time.

As the book of Hebrews explains, He came to the Heavenly Altar as the Most High Priest, offering His own blood as the perfect, sinless sacrifice before Me.

He Who knew no sin of his own became sin (2 Cor. 5:21) and bore the suffering of My wrath on sin.

All of My anger against the disobedience of the whole human race—every person who ever lived before that time and everyone who would ever be born—was unleashed upon His obedience to fulfil My will to the death. His suffering of My vengeance was so great that it clouded His ability to see Me and to know My great love for Him and He cried out the words of Psalm 22, "My God, my God, why hast thou forsaken me?"

Sin clouds one's ability to see and know Me. He had never experienced that before. He suffered all the sin of mankind and He suffered My wrath and vengeance. No one had ever suffered or ever will suffer like My obedient Son! He was made perfect by His sufferings (Hebrews 2:10). His perfection was not only His sinlessness, but also His bearing of total sin and My total wrath! His perfect obedience to My will was sufficient to erase and eradicate Adam's disobedience and that of all his descendants!

For this reason I freely forgive all confessed and repented sin. The miseries of the earth are all related to unrepented, unconfessed sin. As you remit sins by covering them with His blood and redeem the land, you are "showing forth" the sacrificial death of My Lamb; you are extending the borders of His Kingdom until He comes to rule and reign with a rod of iron.

Any sin that is not brought under His blood will be brought under My wrath. It is a very great offence to me when people refuse My gift of forgiveness I extended to mankind when I sent My Son.

Please raise up believers, disciples who will remit sins, redeem the Land and bring souls into My Kingdom, lest they and the other inhabitants of the land unnecessarily suffer the tragic consequences of My unatoned wrath upon their disobedience! When you redeem and remit,[14] you are paving the way for the outpouring of My goodness that will bring sinners to repentance (Romans 2:4).

---

14 See *Redeeming the Land* by Gwen Shaw and *Crosswise* by Henry Gruver, available from engeltalpress.com or by calling (870) 446-2665.

From My Journal:
I Am Brooding

I Am brooding over the earth and I Am brooding over you. As a hen sits on her nest, keeping her eggs warm while they develop into chicks, I Am maintaining the right climate for the development of end-time events and the development of My end-time handmaidens and servants.

I Am so close to you! And you are so barely aware. I spoke through Dr. Smith to you two days ago to open your eyes about the common ground between fear and faith: "they both 'see' something that hasn't happened yet."

The little chorus that Sister Gwen taught you fits here:

*Faith, mighty faith, the promise sees
And looks to God alone.
Laughs at impossibilities
And cries, "It shall be done!"
And cries, and cries, "It shall be done!"
And cries, "It shall be done!"
Laughs at impossibilities
And cries, "It shall be done!"*

Your job is to cry out the truth, the veracity, of the promises I show you.

Don't speak of the dark threats that your enemy shows you, for what you speak will begin to form from your very words. Speak instead My Word, My heart, My mind, My vision, My light, My salvation, My deliverance, My redemption, My soon return, My arising and shining in you. For just as the sun is arising over the mountain on your horizon [this was being written at daybreak], My Light, My Presence as the Sun of Righteousness is arising to turn the darkness of night into the glorious Day of the Lord.

The King is coming. You won't need presidents and prime ministers, and earthly kings, queens, and governors. My Kingdom shall rule ALL the earth and My knowledge of My glory shall cover the earth as the waters cover the sea!

I respond with this prayer:

O Lord, there is nothing You cannot do! I declare Your greatness and power—ability and authority! I say thank You for Your super abundant provision, especially for those who feel trapped by what they call a "fixed income." Lord, please forgive us for limiting You in so many ways! We release our limiting thought patterns to You to erase and re-write. Re-establish our thought patterns to declare Your greatness, love and super-abundant provision for healing, restoration and miraculous, supernatural supply, and for using us for Your Kingdom in spirit, soul and body! Come and rule the "video screen" of our imaginations! AMEN!

A China Connection

Around 2008, Sister Gwen met Annie, a Chinese lady, at a Presidential Prayer Breakfast in Washington, DC. She asked Annie if she were from Inner Mongolia. Surprised, Annie said, "Yes."

"Do you know where the Wang Ye Fu[15] is?"

Even more surprised, Annie said, "I was born in the Wang Ye Fu!"

That started a long conversation and relationship that culminated fulfilling a dream for Sister Gwen. She had always wanted to go back to the places in China where she had been in the late 1940's, and Annie did the *shiang egeh bangfa* to make it happen!

---

15 *Wang Ye Fu*–the palace of the Mongolian *Wang Ye* or prince.

I'm Sticking With You Like Glue!

Through the years I tried to write poems for Sister Gwen for her birthday and Mother's Day. The following is the one I wrote for her on the occasion of her 87th birthday in 2011.

When Elijah said to Elisha,
"Stay in Gilgal, to Bethel I go,"
He replied, "As the Lord and you live, Sir,
Not so, not so, not so!
For as long as you are walking,
On this earth, and the sky is blue,
Though the prophets say you are leaving,
I'm sticking with you like glue!"

When I was a stubborn young maiden,
Plowing in my field of school,
You came and threw your shawl on me,
And I left it to come to your rule.
I've labored these years with you joyful
To be helping you publish your books,
And your magazines, letters and website,
And filling time's crannies and nooks.

So now when you say to me, "Sharon,
Stay here, to the nations I go,"
I reply, "As the Lord and you live, Mum,
Not so, not so, not so!"

For as long as you are walking
On this earth, or in flight in the blue,
Regardless of the prophet's sayings,
I'm sticking with you like glue!

For you see, Sister Gwen, I love you,
And my destiny's twined up in yours,
To carry God's Word and devotion,
Dedication and love to all shores.

So remember, *e'*en when you send me,
To nations now without you,
For the love of God and of you, Sister Gwen,
I'm sticking with you like glue!

"You Have to Love Canada"

Before we went to China with Sister Gwen in 2011, the Lord graced me with another 21-day fast. It had been a few years since I had completed one of that length. I have had some trouble with low blood sugar through the years, so I know when God gives me a fast, it is something sovereign. I felt that it was necessary to fast to help me step up to receive the next level of anointing and impartation from Sister Gwen in my life.

On our way to China, we stopped in Calgary, Alberta, Canada at the Women on the Frontlines Conference, where Sister Gwen had been invited to minister. She celebrated her 87th birthday at that event and just before she ministered that night, she asked me to come up and sing. I felt it was appropriate to sing the song the Lord had given me for her on her 80th birthday.

I Want to Hold You

Chorus
I want to hold you;
Wrap you in My everlasting arms.
I am so near you.
I look into your face;
I long for your embrace,
I want to hold you.

My Bride, I see you.
I know your ev'ry heartbeat
And your love for Me.
My Love, I care for you,

171

Each care you care I bear,
My Bride so fair. (Chorus)

My Bride, I hear you.
Each thought, each prayer you breathe
Goes in My very heart.
My Love, I answer you,
One day so soon you'll see,
It's all from Me.

Bridge
O come alone with Me.
I'll open your eyes to see
This life with all it's care
Is My gift to you to prepare
For all eternity. (Chorus)

My Bride, I want you.
I smell the fragrance of your heartfelt
Praise to Me.
My Love, I long for you.
Receive what now I pour
There's more in store. (Bridge and Chorus)

When I finished singing, Sister Gwen called me to come and kneel beside her. Then she laid her hands on me and "passed the torch" to me. She also commanded me to love Canada like she did. I was so thankful that the Lord had seen to it that I loved Canada from my childhood, having lived so near it (only about 55 miles). Then she had the ministers come and lay hands on me. I was deeply moved.

Her "Swan Song" Trip

For security reasons, I won't go into all the details of the trip, but six of us went with her. We visited the place where she had lived in a mud house in Inner Mongolia. A lady in the

172

church looked at her and said, "I remember you! My mother invited you to our house, and you loved to eat her *jiao tse!*" We knew this was proof positive that the lady was telling the truth. *Jiao tse* (dumplings or "pot stickers") is Sister Gwen's favorite Chinese food!

As the tour was being put together, plans were made for me to go to Japan to be with ETH Ruth Ester Währer, a Swiss missionary. Then a few days more were added so that Sister Gwen could see the Bible School where she taught. The Lord sovereignly led the team there. It was glorious for them to find the Faithful souls who have upheld the Kingdom of God even at times in hostile circumstances! None of the Bible School students that she trained had been martyred, and they continue to preach the Gospel. How wonderful it was to find that her prayers for them over many years were answered!

That was Sister Gwen's final overseas journey. She went full circle, starting and ending her missionary career in China. What a trooper she was!

More of Southeast Asia

From Japan I went to Hong Kong for six days, ministering with Linda Hartzell in fellowships and doing one-on-one ministry, blessing the Lord's saints in that amazing city.

The last nation of the trip was the Philippines. Tommy Schmidt was there also. We ministered with ETH&S Celia and Donald Soriano in three venues in Mindanao and Luzon, each of us preaching one to three times daily.

Upon returning home, we jumped right into the End-Time Handmaidens and Servants "Harvest Gathering" event on November 9. It was a glorious time of worship and preaching of the word of God. Sister Gwen got sick after she came home from China, so again I had to step in for her. It was the first time that I was responsible to emcee a series of meetings. The pressure

Receiving prayer as Sister Gwen
passed the torch to me at
Women on the Frontlines in Can[...]

In front of one of the buildings
of the *Wang Ye Fu* i

The Chinese had just finished refurbishing
the *Wang Ye Fu* in time for their October 1
national day (Sister Gwen's birthday), the
same month we arrived. They even made
wax figures of the royal family to make it look
real. Sister Gwen was shocked to see the
prince again, and enjoyed sitting in his chair.

This is the lady that
remembered Sister Gwen
from her time in Inner
Mongolia 63 years earlier.

was intense as I had only had a day and a half to rest from my journey and jetlag was a challenge. Sister Gwen's condition made it emotionally draining as well. We didn't know if she might slip across into eternity while we were holding the meetings.

Declining Health

She finally went to the doctor after Christmas and he put her in the hospital. The x-ray of her heart showed that it was enlarged about five or six times its normal size. Dr. Ron Revard, her cardiologist and friend, put her on oxygen 24/7. Thankfully, she recovered enough to make a few more short journeys.

She had been diagnosed with congestive heart failure about twenty years earlier. Statistics show that seven out of ten die within ten years of being diagnosed. She was on her third pacemaker! Through the years she had rightly earned the nickname of, "the Energizer Bunny." In the office, we called her "The White Tornado"!

Her Last World Convention

In the last couple of months before our 2012 World Convention, Sister Gwen asked the staff, "Do you know of any scripture in the Bible where God told Moses to take the Children of Israel into the Promised Land?" None of us could and she researched the answer to her question carefully.

At the World Convention, after I preached a message on "Ask God for the Nations as Your Inheritance," she stepped up to the pulpit and said, "The Lord told me that I was to do something, and I believe this is the time. You have just heard, God willing, your next president of the End-Time Handmaidens and Servants speak.[16] And the Lord told me that I was to impart

16 A video clip of this incident is on our website: endtimehandmaidens.org. Hold the mouse over "About Us" and click on "Sharon Buss – Our President."

to Sharon and Phil the gifts and anointing that's on my life. My anointing that's on me came on me in many ways, but a special anointing came in the Philippines, when I read Aimee Semple McPherson's book, *This Is That…* I got such a burden. I wanted this same anointing…the calling of God on my life is so great—I needed it…"

She related how Evelyn Thompson, a Four Square Missionary in Mindanao had received the laying on of Sister Aimee's hands. Sister Aimee asked Evelyn if she wanted the same anointing in her life, and was able to accept the persecution, trials, testings, the lies, false accusations, and all the hardships that will come with it. Evelyn responded, "By God's Grace." Sister Aimee laid hands on Evelyn, prayed for her and passed it on. Years later, when Sister Gwen was hungry for that same anointing, Evelyn imparted it to her because the Lord told her to.

Sister Gwen then said, "This is a package deal, you know! You get it all—not just the Glory—you also get the abasement!

"So I am a spiritual granddaughter of Aimee Semple McPherson." And turning to me she said, "And today, I'm passing that anointing on to you. That makes you the [great] granddaughter."

Philip came to the pulpit to join me. Then she read Deuteronomy 31:7-8, "'And Moses called unto Joshua, and said unto him in the sight of all Israel, Be strong and of a good courage: for thou must go with this people unto the land which the LORD hath sworn unto their fathers to give them; and thou shalt cause them to inherit it. And the LORD, he it is that doth go before thee; he will be with thee, he will not fail thee, neither forsake thee: fear not, neither be dismayed.' There will be battles, especially at the beginning. " She went on to read Deuteronomy 34:9, "'And Joshua the son of Nun was full of the spirit of wisdom; for Moses had laid his hands upon him: and

---

Click on the link "Sister Gwen imparting her anointing to Sharon."

the children of Israel hearkened unto him, and did as the LORD commanded Moses.' Now there's some powerful authority in transference of impartation with the laying on of hands.

"Paul said to Timothy in 2 Timothy 1:6, 'Wherefore I put thee in remembrance that thou stir up the gift of God, which is in thee by the putting on of my hands.'

"God's hand is upon you to send you unto Pharaohs and bring the people out of Egypt. Now God never promised Moses to take them into the Promised Land. He promised him to take them out of Egypt. God doesn't make a promise to break it. We say, 'Well why? Was it only because he lost his temper?' Well partly so, but it was already not ordained from long before. God had not promised Moses that He would bring them into the Promised Land—only that He would deliver them out of Egypt. I got you out with the help of the Holy Ghost, Who did it through my life." Then turning to us said, "But you will bring them in, and you'll see things I never saw, hallelujah." Then turning back to the congregation, she said, "And so will all of you. Praise God!"

Then anointing us with oil and laying hands on us, she said, "Receive the anointing, the impartation that was given to Aimee Semple McPherson. Fulfil the work. Finish the job. Receive the anointing that's in my life, and hold it pure before God all the days of your lives, in the name of the Father, Son and the Holy Ghost. In the name of Jesus, receive the anointing—the impartation of the Holy Ghost in your life."

Another Setback and Recovery

Sister Gwen was so determined to participate in the World Convention, that she did not take her medications as she should. This resulted in a flare-up of congestive swelling that progressed into pneumonia, and she was hospitalized. Philip

177

and I were in Texas at the time on a ministry trip with a group from China. I had a great peace that this was not her appointed time and that she would be all right.

From the hospital, she entered Hillcrest, a Mennonite nursing home in Harrison, Arkansas, for rehabilitation. Sister Gwen has always been a night owl, but she took this as an assignment from the Lord to a different kind of mission field. She was a great blessing to the patients and staff. She remained there for six weeks, regaining her strength in time to teach in our ISOM on the subject of Revival.

During that school I had my first opportunity to teach. The Lord gave me the subject, "God and Sons, Wonder Working Company." It was an exciting subject. I hope to get the study made into a book.

Overseas Again

Philip and I were invited to be a part of a group that went to Argentina to minister in November of 2012. Linda Hartzell, Mark Bristow, Maurice and Devorah Sklar, Claren and Nancy McQueen, and several of Pastor Mark's ministry team were there. The Holy Spirit was poured out in a mighty way with many healings and transformed lives.

From there we went to Japan for two weeks with ETH Ruth Ester Währer. It was early December and we were able to join in on her annual Christmas concerts. Christmas is an excellent time to introduce "the reason for the season" to people who know nothing about Jesus or Christianity.

Then we flew to China for an event where we were able to help in the flow of something the Holy Spirit was doing.

Her Last Christmas

We arrived home at 11:00 p.m. December 23 after eighteen flights in the journey. We were just in time for Sister Gwen's last

"The End of the World"
The southern tip of South America
in Argentina

We sang in the church
that Ruth Ester Währer
pastors in Japan.

I discovered that
I enjoy Japanese food
with Ruth Ester and
Ai San

I came to love the Chinese flag
when I saw the Christians
using it in worship

Dancing in my Indian *sari* in China

Christmas on earth. It snowed on Christmas Day, so we moved the festivities to her house so she wouldn't have to go out in the cold. In spite of her frailty, she was a real trooper and gave the last of her strength to the celebrations with her family and staff.

She pulled on God for the strength to speak to the young people at our annual Anointed Youth Retreat. She ministered on New Year's Eve as she normally did—and it was powerful, even though she was weak in her body.

The Final Decline

It was a huge blessing to me to get to spend some time with Sister Gwen in her last three weeks. I spent a number of nights with her because her primary care giver, Doreen Shurley, had her dad here for Christmas. When he went home, Doreen had to step in to help with the year-end inventory in the bookstore.

Sister Gwen continued to grow weaker, yet she kept trying to get up and get dressed, even if it was only for a couple of hours.

At one time, she was believing God to help her reach the age of ninety. About a week before she passed on, I asked her, "Sister Gwen, do you want us to continue to believe God with you to help you hit ninety?"

"Not like this!" she retorted. She said that she basically felt fine, but just hated feeling weak.

Are YOU Ready?

A couple of nights before she crossed over into Glory, Sister Gwen spoke up about 4:15 a.m. and excitedly said, "Jim Shaw! I see Jim Shaw!"

Myrna asked, "Is he coming for you?"

She replied, "He's coming for all of us. He's calling us to come. We need to get prepared. *I'm* ready. Are **you** ready?"

Rona asked, "Do you see Jesus?"

At first she said, "No." Then she said, "He's coming for us all **now**. Praise God! Hallelujah!"

When we talked about the incident in the morning, we were reminded of what Jesus said recently to a sister who saw Him in a vision: "Don't say anymore that I'm coming soon. Tell them I'm coming NOW!"

Sister Gwen's pointed words have been ringing in my ears— she was looking at me when she spoke them: "*I'm* ready. Are **you** ready?"

Glory

Sister Gwen passed into the Presence of the Lord on January 13, 2013 at 1:30 p.m. It was hard to let her go, but she had told us so many times, "Next time, don't pray me back!"

Linda Hartzell said that she felt the angel who was to escort her home arrive in the house at 9:40 that morning. Interestingly, the grandfather clock in the living room stopped at that precise time. Thankfully, it did run again after Rona started it up again, not like the clock in the old song.

We discussed it together that sometimes you can feel the spirit of a loved one linger for a while, but not Sister Gwen. It was as though when she saw the Gate of Heaven begin to open to her, she shot through it, and never looked back!

About 24 hours before Sister Gwen passed, I was walking through the front door of her house and a song came welling up in my spirit:

You Were Born For This Day.
You were born for this day.
You were born for this hour.
You were born for such a time as this (2x)

Verse 1
God has raised up a people to fulfil His ev'ry Word
That's been spoken by the prophets for these end times.
You will walk through the fire,
You will pass through the flood.
The destructions shall not harm you
In the secret place of His blood.

Verse 2
God will pour out His Spirit upon all flesh
And His servants and His Handmaidens shall prophesy.
They shall run like the mighty
In the strength of His breath
And their fasting and their prayer
Shall deliver souls from death.

Chorus 2
I was born for this day.
I was born for this hour.
I was born for such a time as this. (2x)

Doreen Shurley wrote this song for our World Convention in 2011 and I helped with the lyrics. We've been using it as the theme song for our Friday night Live Worship service that we stream live to our website. Little did I know that when it came up in my spirit that afternoon, that this was the day for which I was born.

"Move into This House..."

A year or two before she passed, Sister Gwen and I were standing in her bedroom when she sternly gave me a strict order, "I want you to move into this house the same day that I die. I want you sleeping in this room that night."

Through the kindness of the Lord, that same thought had come up in my spirit just a few days earlier, so it wasn't as much of a shock to me as it might have been.

So in the late evening of Sister Gwen's graduation day, when we had finished making multitudes of arrangements and telephone calls, Philip and I went back to our house to get a few things we would need to begin to settle into the Manor. When we arrived back in our new room, and I set down the bags I had brought, I looked at the clock. It was midnight. I rejoiced in my spirit that we had somehow made it by an important deadline.

I had already been staying there quite a bit, so it wasn't as difficult a transition for me as it was for Philip. This was a suddenly and we simply had to step up to the challenge.

Most of the time when you move into a new house, it's empty, and you bring your belongings and move in. Sister Gwen's house was full of her belongings, so we had to do a good bit of shifting to make room for ourselves. Philip has been wonderful at organizing and putting things in order, and I am so grateful!

So I have come full circle to live again in the first house where I stayed when I came to Engeltal. So much has changed. We had to add on to it when Sister Gwen could no longer climb stairs, so it is much bigger than it was then.

I am really quite awed. Sister Gwen asked me once, "What are you going to change when I'm gone?"

I told her honestly, "I'm not thinking about it." I didn't want to; I felt it was inappropriate. So, we are just taking one step at a time in the grace and mercy of the Lord.

Under the Yoke

Now that Sister Gwen has gone on to glory, I still see myself just "under the yoke," only now it is much larger and more elaborate. Some months ago, I was meditating on how Jesus dwells in us and we dwell in Him, and pictured myself clothed in Jesus. His shoulders happened to be six inches taller than mine—so I know Who is really carrying the yoke.

Sister Gwen's greatest desire was to simply obey the Lord, and she taught that principle to us. We intend to keep that as our highest goal.

Now What?

In her challenging article called "Share My Burden," Sister Gwen tells of her experience when she was being gloriously used of God in Argentina in 1966:

> Throughout Argentina I had seen the mighty hand of God working with signs following the preaching of His Word. It was there in Buenos Aires one night that something happened which would change many lives. I had just ministered in a large Assembly of God Church. God had poured out His Spirit. Miracles of healing had taken place. People had seen angels. God had come down to be with us. As I went to my lonely hotel room that night, tired and exhausted, I lay on my bed. I looked up to God and asked Him a question. "God, how can you use me? I am nothing. I make mistakes. I am far from perfect. Yet I have seen Your glory like a trail of fire following me everywhere. How? Why?

184

He answered me! "It's because you are willing to do anything I ask you to do!"

"Is that all, Lord? Then You could use anyone, any woman, who, like myself, would be totally surrendered to You!"

"Yes, My child, I could," He answered.

"Then, Lord, raise up ten thousand women— women just like myself, who will pay any price, make any sacrifice, be totally obedient to Your will."

The Word of the Lord to Sister Gwen in 1970 was, "You are raised up of God to call out the End-Time Handmaidens." So here we are! We've been called out. We are a mighty army of women and men who, like Sister Gwen, have declared our willingness to surrender totally to the will of God and obey Him in whatever He asks. We will go on carrying the torch that she has passed to us.

In the New Testament, the Greek word *apokalupto* is translated into English with the word "reveal," but it means "to uncover, lay open what has been veiled or covered up disclose, make bare, to make known, make manifest, disclose what before was unknown."[17]

A related word, *apokalupsis* is the one that is translated "manifestation" in Romans 8:19, "For the earnest expectation of the creature waiteth for the manifestation of the sons of God." It is also the word translated "revelation" in Revelation 1:1, "The Revelation of Jesus Christ..." It could be literally translated "to take the lid off." I keep hearing the words, *apokalupto* and *apokalupsis* in my spirit with regard to what God is doing now in the earth.

---

17 Thayer and Smith. "Greek Lexicon entry for Apokalupto". "The NAS New Testament Greek Lexicon". . 1999. http://www.biblestudytools.com/lexicons/greek/nas/apokalupto.html

One of the next events on God's schedule is the revelation of Himself in His people. God is planning to bring to the light those of His children who have been pressing in to know Him and to allow Him to cut away the fleshly nature in a circumcision of the heart. He has been working in many, many hidden lives to help them to "partake of the divine nature" (2 Peter 1:4). His Holy Spirit is available to all of us to transform us into His image as we follow on to know Him

Sister Gwen was such a wonderful person—almost bigger than life! And when the Lord took her home, it was as though a great lid was removed, and we are discovering what a huge army of the Lord was being built under her. It's an army of obedient soldiers who are listening to their Commander for orders and are acting upon them.

It's time now for the army to discover the army! We need to get to know one another and connect with the network that God has in place.

Now Therefore Arise, Go Over This Jordan

The final night of our first Branch Officers Convocation without Sister Gwen, the Lord put it on my heart to share from the book of Joshua. Several speakers during the Holy Convocation we held in honour of the works the Lord did through Sister Gwen's life, referred to the first chapter of Joshua, verse 2: "Moses my servant is dead; now therefore arise, go over this Jordan, thou, and all this people, unto the land which I do give to them, even to the children of Israel." That's where I began my message about how it is time for the End-Time Handmaidens and Servants to now arise and cross over into our Promised Land.

186

The Lord has promised us the nations as we have asked them of Him according to Psalm 2:8. He has promised us revival in many prophetic words and in our theme scripture, Acts 2:17-18, "And it shall come to pass in the last days, saith God, I will pour out of my Spirit upon all flesh: and your sons and your daughters shall prophesy, and your young men shall see visions, and your old men shall dream dreams: And on my servants and on my handmaidens I will pour out in those days of my Spirit; and they shall prophesy."

Let us cross over the "Jordan River" of limitations to receive the double portion anointing for revival and the nations!

The Lord proved Himself to the Children of Israel as they obeyed Him in following the Ark of the Covenant where they had never gone before, crossing the flooding Jordan River on dry ground because the Lord had rolled back the waters.

When they made their camp and celebrated their first Passover in the Promised Land, the Lord commanded that Joshua make "sharp knives" to circumcise the young warriors that had been born while they wandered in the wilderness. The Bible doesn't explain why they hadn't been circumcised since the Exodus from Egypt, but it wasn't right for them to inherit the Land given to them by the covenant of the Lord to Abraham, Isaac, and Jacob if they didn't have the sign of the covenant in their bodies. The excess flesh has to be cut away before we can possess the promises. Let us seek the face of the Lord to help us get free from whatever is keeping us from walking in the Covenant promises and possessing our Promised Land.

I would like to quote 2 Peter 1:3-8. "According as His divine power hath given unto us all things that pertain unto life and godliness, through the knowledge of him that hath called us to glory and virtue: Whereby are given unto us exceeding great and precious promises: that by these ye might be partakers of the divine nature, having escaped the corruption that is in the world through lust. And beside this, giving all diligence, add to

187

your faith virtue; and to virtue knowledge; And to knowledge temperance; and to temperance patience; and to patience godliness; And to godliness brotherly kindness; and to brotherly kindness charity. For if these things be in you, and abound, they make you that ye shall neither be barren nor unfruitful in the knowledge of our Lord Jesus Christ."

We must press in for the precious promises to walk in the Divine nature. We are in Him and He dwells in us. Let the Holy Spirit cut away everything that doesn't look like Him.

A magnifying glass can only magnify if it is transparent. The more transparent we are, the more the Lord who dwells within us will be magnified.

Grace to Overcome

Sometimes I still have my momentary meltdowns, my eyes filling with tears, or outright sobbing when I think about Sister Gwen. I might say, "Oh Mama!" and hold onto something that reminds me of her. Mourning is a process.

The highlights I have shared in this book don't include the many mundane days of just plain work, and I've saved a few thoughts for other books that I have on my heart. I haven't had the time or space to tell of all the mission trips and Bible Lands tours we accomplished. I haven't told about the joys of becoming grandparents to Mia Rain Saller and Lucas Braiden Saller who are four and a half and two and a half at the time of this writing.

I haven't told all there is to tell about myself. I am certainly just as human as you are, dear reader. My sins would certainly have taken me to Hell if the mercy of God had not intervened. I'm convinced that we all have the potential to fall into any degradation and commit any sin.

I've always tried to practice what Sister Gwen preached and she taught the life of overcoming—I haven't told you my struggles to overcome, but know that I have struggled. Sometimes I won the battle and sometimes I lost, but the grace of God was always there for me when I repented. This grace will enable you to win your battle, too, no matter how difficult it is.

The following is from my journal:

I heard in my spirit, "But we have this treasure in earthen vessels" (2 Corinthains 4:7), and at the same time, I saw in my mind's eye the Dead Sea Scrolls in the Qumran cave, "that the excellency of the power may be of God and not of us."

The treasure in My Presence, My Word, is within. Don't look to the exterior of the vessel and judge the contents. "Man looketh upon the outward appearance, but God looketh upon the heart."

Leave My vessels to Me. As long as you continue to have shortcomings and areas in which you have not yet overcome, and you continue to walk in the limitations of unglorified flesh, be careful how you judge others who have not yet overcome.

I am patient with you and have gained much ground in you; some was taken little by little and some all at once.

You keep asking Me to teach you My ways. I have brought this case in point into your midst to show you another facet of My character and how I deal with hearts. Keep watching and keep learning. I am well able to use earthen vessels to pour out My Glory.

At times, I use contentious preachers to preach My Gospel and bring souls into My Kingdom. Sometimes they are all I have to work with.

Walk humbly before Me. I want to teach you by My Spirit the difference between the discernment that comes by My

answer to prayer! rent the house! (handwritten)

Spirit and the judgment that comes by the letter of the law. Be careful not to be a Pharisee. Let My love be your standard.

10:35 AM (handwritten)
1/22/15 (handwritten)

I see the finished vessel—you see the lump of clay. Leave My lumps of clay to Me. Don't speak what you see with your natural eyes. Speak My mercy and grace and I will show It. Speak My eternal purposes and I will bring them to pass.

I have given you a privilege to show mercy and love to one of My imperfect vessels. You will receive back that which you have given, pressed down, shaken together and running over.

Isn't it amazing what I can do with imperfect vessels?! The excellency of the power is mine. I will do what pleases Me. If you watch humbly, I'll let you see My processes. If you watch proudly, you'll only see the truth in the end.

You Were Born for This Day

When the Board of Directors met to elect officers and a new Board member, Sister Gwen's appointment of me to the office of the president was confirmed. And just like Papa Jim served as the Vice President/Treasurer, we elected Philip to that position. Arla Dill serves as the Secretary, Emmanuel Jibuike and Catherine James serve as Board Members. Philip and I are so very grateful to our Board for their wisdom and guidance. They hear from the Lord, and will continue to help us at the helm.

I'm so excited to see what God is going to do! We celebrate Sister Gwen's life, and carry on to water all the good seed she sowed. The future of the ministry she founded continues to be in the hands of Almighty God as it always was.

Amen

Appendix

The following are two articles written for our prayer letter and website that I felt should be included.

What is an End-Time Handmaiden?

An End-Time Handmaiden is one who has a call of God on her life to serve Him unconditionally with trusting obedience. She surrenders her will to Him and joyfully takes up His instead. She joins Jesus in the Garden of Gethsemane and says with Him, "Not my will, but Thine be done." She takes up her cross and follows Him.

She surrenders her right to eat as she enters a 21-day fast to receive the double-portion anointing to which she is called.

She is an intercessor and learns how to pray the prayers that are on the heart of the Chief Intercessor, Jesus Christ.

She has a burden for the nations and will weep for souls, travailing with Paul "until Christ be formed" in them.

Every Kindred, Every Tribe

She may be of any race, kindred, tongue or tribe, but she loves and serves Jesus as Her Bridegroom and soon-coming King. She may differ in many ways in her culture and physical appearance from other End-Time Handmaidens—she may be tall or short, large or small, young or old, in a wheelchair or strong, but she perseveres in prayer and brings forth the fruit of the Kingdom of God in the earth.

She knows with Paul that she is in a relay race and carries the baton with faithfulness to her calling, ready to pass it on to the next generation when her lap is finished.

She may be called to preach or she may be hidden in the prayer closet. She may travel to another nation and spend the rest of her life serving the Lord there or she may make many short trips to mission fields, coming home to work and raise money for her next journey, or she may simply travel on her knees, touching souls by her intercessions. She may be called to the church or the streets or the workplace, but she knows she's called. And if she fails or falls, she knows to repent and get up and go on to fulfil her destiny.

She may be an apostle, a prophetess, an evangelist, pastor or teacher, or she may be a prayer warrior. She may be a doctor, attorney, teacher, nurse, computer technician, housewife, real estate agent, student, pilot, flight attendant, cook or mayor. The call manifests in many ways. She blooms where she is planted. She has a call to press into God and go beyond the limitations of her natural circumstances into the limitlessness of His Kingdom.

She is a worshipper. Whether she can sing in tune or not, whether she can dance with rhythm and beauty in man's eyes or not, whether she can play an instrument or not, her heart is toward her Beloved Bridegroom and to Him her "voice is sweet and her countenance is comely."

She may be loud and bombastic or quiet and subdued—or both, depending on the move of the Holy Spirit. End-Time Handmaidens are all individuals and diverse—each one is unique. They all bear a certain mark of a calling of God in their spirit.

Raised up of God
to call out the End-Time Handmaidens

Sister Gwen Shaw received a call of God in her youth and was a missionary to China, going there by faith in 1947 with only $10 in her pocket and no promise of support. When China closed, she continued to work in Taiwan and Hong Kong for

192

many years. In 1963, she was led by the Lord to fast for 21 days and the Lord gave her a double portion anointing. She began to go to the nations and a trail of revival fire followed her wherever she went. She went many times to India, her great love. She wanted to lay her life down for the Lord in the Himalayan Mountains, her love for India was so great. But one day while walking down the street in New Delhi, the Lord spoke to her and asked, "Would you be willing to lay down your desire to be a martyr for Me in the Himalayas?"

She responded, "Lord, I have given you everything—do I have to give up my heart's desire too?"

"But, what if I have a better plan for you? Would you be willing?"

Knowing she could trust Him, she agreed.

In 1970, when she was on a water fast, Sister Gwen received the word of the Lord from a prophet of God. He said that an angel met him and told him to go to her and give her the word that "She is raised up of God to call out the End-Time Handmaidens."

Sympathetic Vibrations

Have you ever been around a piano when a loud noise happens? If someone shouts or sings loudly, or if something is dropped and it causes a loud sound, the string or strings that have the same wave length as that sound will begin to vibrate in "sympathy" with that sound. You will hear the piano or other stringed instrument echoing back.

The same principle applies in the spirit. When you get around someone who has the same calling in God that you have, your spirit responds with a resounding "Yes!" and you know that God's eternal purposes are somehow involved with that encounter.

If you have heard Sister Gwen speak or you have read her articles or books and you feel something deep in your spirit saying, "Yes!," then you might be an End-Time Handmaiden. If you are a man and you feel the same resounding "Yes!," then you might be an End-Time Servant. It takes a very special, humble, strong man to be willing to join himself to these anointed sisters in the Lord.

You Are Not an Island

If you find you have been reading a description of yourself, you need to know that you are not an island; you are a part of a vast network. God wants you to join yourself to others of "like precious faith" and calling. Come to the events the Lord is calling you to (Officers Retreat, Winter Camp, World Convention, local branch meetings). Get connected to the support system—you need us and we need you. You are not alone. Just like Elijah found out that he was not alone in his ministry to God and that there were 7,000 who had not bowed their knee to Baal, you must find the fellowship of those with a calling like your own and be encouraged to be all God has called you to be.

— Sharon Buss

What Is an End-Time Servant?

An End-Time Servant comes out of a special class of men. Not many men are humble enough to come under a name like End-Time Handmaidens, or not look sheepish when asked "You're an End-Time Handmaiden?" It takes a special class of man to support his wife, or a woman in ministry, that could perhaps have more anointing than he does, and to release her to fulfill the call of God on her life, and not to be jealous of her giftings.

An End-Time Servant is one who will "follow the Lamb withersoever He goeth" (Revelation 14:4). An End-Time Servant is one who is called to be a King and a Priest. He will walk like David did, a man after God's own heart. He will walk as a man of integrity in all areas of his life, both in the spiritual and in the natural. He will walk in holiness before the Lord pressing upward into the high calling of Christ Jesus. He is strengthened by the Lord to endure all temptations, knowing that satan also has a passion for souls, his included.

He will be a worshiper, crying out for a deeper relationship with the Lord and more of His glory. Isaiah 26:9a says, "With my soul have I desired thee in the night; yea, with my spirit within me will I seek thee early…"

I want to encourage the men to "not let the footmen weary you," Jeremiah 12:5. It is time to press in to be as one of God's Horsemen, in order to cross the "swelling of Jordan" or to combat problems that are thrown at us on a day to day basis.

When you took your vows and had Sister Gwen lay hands on you, you had an impartation given to you of this ministry "to do the Will of the Father." There are many ministries out there doing much for the kingdom, and so many attractions to them, but I ask you to remember the land of your calling and not to forget Sister Gwen, who has paid for the "pearl of Great

Price" by her life, which is imparted into you. I encourage you to pay the price, and come worship the Lord with us, and press in to what God has for us in the upcoming meetings. Don't miss hearing what the Holy Ghost will be speaking to you. "I must by all means keep this feast that cometh in Jerusalem..." (Acts 18:21).

So please come to the Feasts of the Lord in our events.

— Philip Buss

TAKE THE LID OFF

Life-Changing Books by Gwen R. Shaw

UNCONDITIONAL SURRENDER. Gwen Shaw's life story. Paperback ....#000102
.... • French #000102FR
DVD UNCONDITIONAL SURRENDER NTSC (North American format) ....#DGSN
DVD UNCONDITIONAL SURRENDER PAL (European format) ....#DGSP

Devotional Books

DAILY PREPARATIONS FOR PERFECTION ....Softcover #000202
    French ....Softcover #000202FR
DAY BY DAY— *A devotional based on the Psalms* .... • Softcover #000204
.... • Hardcover #000203
    French..................................... • Softcover #000204FR • Hardcover #000203FR
    German.. • Softcover #000204GE
FROM THE HEART OF JESUS — *A devotional based on the Words of Jesus.*
....Hardcover #000207
GEMS OF WISDOM — *A daily devotional based on the book of Proverbs.*
....Hardcover #000209
    French.. • Hardcover #000209FR
IN THE BEGINNING — *A daily devotional based on the book of Genesis.*
....Hardcover #000211
    French.. • Hardcover #000211FR

Classic Bible Studies

BEHOLD THE BRIDEGROOM COMETH! A Bible study on the soon return of Jesus Christ.
....#000304 • Italian #000304IT • Russian #000304RU
ENDUED WITH LIGHT TO REIGN FOREVER. Bible study on the eternal, supernatural,
creative light of God...#000306 • French #000306FR
GOD'S END-TIME BATTLE-PLAN. Bible study on spiritual warfare ....#00035
    ....• Spanish #000305SP • French #000305FR • Russian #000305RU
IT'S TIME FOR REVIVAL. A Bible study on revival .... #000311 • French #000311FR
OUR MINISTERING ANGELS. A Bible study on angels.............#000308 • French #000308FR
.... • Russian #000308RU
POUR OUT YOUR HEART. A Bible study on intercessory prayer ....#000301
.... • Spanish #000301SP • French #000301FR
.... • Russian #000301RU • Italian #000301IT • Japanese #000301JA
REDEEMING THE LAND. A Bible study on spiritual warfare..#000309
.... • Spanish #000309SP • French #000309FR • Italian #000309IT
THE FINE LINE. This Bible study on the soul realm and the spirit realm........................#000307
.... French #000307FR
THE POWER OF THE PRECIOUS BLOOD — A Bible study on the Blood of Jesus
.... #000303 • Spanish #000303SP • Chinese #000303CH • French #000303FR
.... • Italian #000303IT • Polish #000303PO • Russian #000303RU
THE POWER OF PRAISE. Bible study on praise ....#000312

197

YE SHALL RECEIVE POWER FROM ON HIGH Bible study on the Baptism of the Holy Spirit.
....#000310 • Chinese #000310CH • Spanish #000310SP
YOUR APPOINTMENT WITH GOD. A Bible study on fasting ....#000302
.... • Spanish #000302SP • Chinese #000302CH • French #000302FR
.... • German #000302GE • Italian #000302IT • Japanese #000302JA • Russian #000302RU

In-Depth Bible Studies

FORGIVE AND RECEIVE. The epistle to Philemon ....#000406
GRACE ALONE. The epistle to the Galatians.......................................#000402
MYSTERY REVEALED. The epistle to the Ephesians ....#000403
OUR GLORIOUS HEAD. The epistle to the Colossians! ....#000404
THE CATCHING AWAY! The books of 1 and 2 Thessalonians.......................#000407
THE LOVE LETTER. The epistle to the Philippians.......................#000405
THE TRIBES OF ISRAEL. Bible Course ....• Binder #000501 • 13 CD set #CTGS1
....• French #000501FR

Women of the Bible Series

EVE—MOTHER OF US ALL ....#000801
SARAH—PRINCESS OF ALL MANKIND ....#000802
REBEKAH—THE BRIDE.......................#000803
LEAH AND RACHEL—THE TWIN WIVES OF JACOB.......................#000804
MIRIAM—THE PROPHETESS ....#000805
DEBORAH AND JAEL. God's "warrior women" ....#000806

Other Books by Gwen Shaw

ASHTORETH: Goddess of Lust ....#000615
GOING HOME.......................#000607 • French #000607FR
KEEPING GOD'S SECRETS.......................#000609
LOVE, THE LAW OF THE ANGELS ....#000601 • Spanish #000601SP
SIGI AND I ....#000614
SONG OF LOVE. The Song of Solomon ....#000401 • French #000401FR
SWORD OF LOVE.......................#000613
THE FALSE FAST ....#000602
THE HIGH WAY OF FORGIVENESS ....#000616
THE LIGHT WILL COME FROM RUSSIA ....#000606
THE PARABLE OF THE GOLDEN RAIN.......................#000603 • French #000603FR
THEY SHALL MOUNT UP WITH WINGS AS EAGLES ....#000604 • French #000604FR
TO BE LIKE JESUS ....#000605

Pocket Sermon Booklets

BEHOLD, THIS DREAMER COMETH ....#000707 • Spanish #000707SP
BORN FOR SUCH A TIME AS THIS.......................#000720
BREAKTHROUGH ....#000708
DON'T STRIKE THE ROCK! ....#000704 • Russian #000704RU • French #000704FR
FROM PEAK TO PEAK ....#000718
GOD WILL DESTROY THE VEIL OF BLINDNESS.......................#000712

TAKE THE LID OFF

HASTENING OUR REDEMPTION ....#000705 • French #000705FR
IT CAN BE AVERTED ....#000706 • Spanish #000706SP
IT'S TIME FOR CHANGE...#000714
KAIROS TIME ....#000709 • Spanish #000709SP
KNOWING ONE ANOTHER IN THE SPIRIT...........................#000703 • French #000703FR
TEACH THEM TO WEEP ....#000716 • French #000716FR
THAT WE MAY BE ONE ....#000715
THE ANOINTING BREAKS THE YOKE ....#000710 • Spanish #000710SP
THE CHANGING OF THE GUARD ....#000719
THE CHURCH OF THE OPEN ARMS ....#000713
THE CRUCIFIED LIFE ....#000701
THE MASTER IS COME AND CALLETH FOR THEE.............#000702 • French #000702FR
THE MERCY SEAT .... #000711
THROW THE HEAD OF SHEBA OVER THE WALL.................................#000717

Books about Heaven

INTRA MUROS (Within the Gates) unabridged — *Rebecca Springer* ....#109101
PARADISE, THE HOLY CITY AND THE GLORY OF THE THRONE ....#104201

Children's Books

LITTLE ONES TO HIM BELONG ....#000901 • Chinese #000901CH
TELL ME THE STORIES OF JESUS ....#000902

Prophecies and Visions

THE DAY OF THE LORD IS NEAR: Vol. I - IV.............................with binder #001000

Music

TREASURES IN SONG Sister Gwen's anointed music in beautiful arrangements. These songs tell her life story! Two pages of full color photos of Sister Gwen in ministry and travels . #000608

Prices are subject to change.
For a complete catalogue with current pricing, contact:

Engeltal Press

P.O. Box 447 • Jasper, ARK 72641 U.S.A.
Telephone (870) 446-2665 • Fax (870) 446-2259
E-mail books@eth-s.org • Website www.EngeltalPress.com

Engeltal Press
P.O. Box 447
Jasper, AR 72641
(870) 446-2665
books@eth-s.org
www.engeltalpress.com

Cover design: Joy Kusek

Printed in the United States of America

Take the Lid Off

The Next Generation of End-Time Handmaidens and Servants

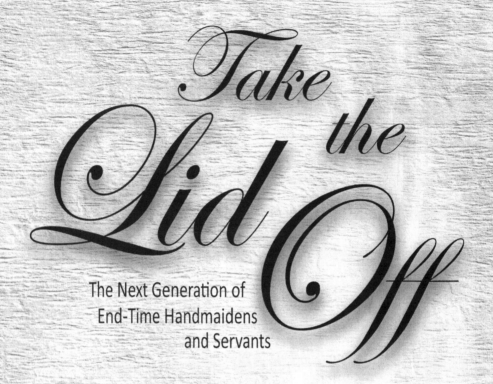

My Story | Sharon Buss